MARCH 16, 2009

TO: CAROLE

MAY YOU ALWAYS REMEMBER THAT "WHEN YOU'RE DOWN TO NOTHING, GOD IS UP TO SOMETHING"

FANTASTIC IN YOUR LIFE!

BLESSINGS,
BARBARA

D1104465

When You're *Down* To Nothing, God Is *Up* To Something

Barbara Washington Franklin

When You're *Down* To Nothing, God Is *Up* To Something

Barbara Washington Franklin

Copyright © 2008 by Barbara Washington Franklin

When You're Down To Nothing, God Is Up To Something
by Barbara Washington Franklin

Printed in the United States of America

ISBN 978-1-60647-120-3

All rights reserved solely by the author. The author guarantees all contents are original and do not infringe upon the legal rights of any other person or work. No part of this book may be reproduced in any form without the permission of the author. The views expressed in this book are not necessarily those of the publisher.

Unless otherwise indicated, Bible quotations are taken from The King James Version of the Bible (KJV), and The Message (MSG), Copyright © 1993, 1994, 1995, 1996, 2000, 2001, 2002, Used by permission of NavPress Publishing Group, and The Holy Bible: New International Version ®, NIV®, Copyright © 1973, 1978, 1984 by International Bible Society, Used by permission of Zondervan, and The Holy Bible, New Living Translation (NLT), Copyright © 1996 by Tyndale House Publishers, Wheaton, Illinois, Used by permission.

Italicized text in Scripture quotations indicates the author's emphasis.

Every effort has been made to give proper credit for all quotations, songs and stories. If, for any reason, proper credit has been omitted, please notify the author or publisher, and proper acknowledgement will be duly given in future printings. Names and details in some anecdotes and illustrations have been changed to protect identities.

Library of Congress Cataloging-in-Publication Data

1. God.   2. Sovereignty   3. Faith   4. Christian Conduct   5. Biblical
                                                              Principles.

I. Title

Cover Photograph Courtesy *Ebony Magazine*

www.xulonpress.com

Dedication

In Humble Obedience to

God,
My Heavenly Father

Jesus Christ,
My Lord and Savior

The Holy Spirit,
My Comforter and Friend

In Deepest Gratitude to

My Mother,
Eunice Vetta Ross Washington

In Loving Remembrance of

My Father,
Robert Benjamin Washington

My Grandmother,
Rosa Lee Bradley Washington Terry

My Husband,
Dr. Hardy R. Franklin

"Must Jesus bear the cross alone and all the world go free?
No, there's a cross for everyone, and
there's a cross for me."

Thomas Shepherd
1665-1739
Must Jesus Bear the Cross Alone

"Whosoever will come after me, let him deny himself,
and take up his cross, and follow me."

Mark 8:34
Holy Bible

"We are born into the world
with our own unique cross to bear.
If we manage to escape our cross today, rest assured,
another one will be waiting to take its place tomorrow.
But if we restrain our escapist inclinations, and this,
admittedly, takes a lot of grit and guts, and begin to see
our personal crucibles as Christ centered, we are guaranteed
the victory of a resurrected life in Christ Jesus."

L.B. (Mrs. Charles E.) Cowman
1870-1960
Streams in the Desert

Nearer, my God, to Thee, nearer to Thee!
E'en though it be a cross that raiseth me,
Still all my song shall be, Nearer, my God, to Thee.

Sarah F. Adams
1805-1848
Nearer, My God, to Thee

"Every man is born into the world to do
something unique and something distinctive, and if he or
she does not do it, it will never be done."

Dr. Benjamin E. Mays
1895-1984

Table of Contents

Introduction

Every life that God intends to use mightily in His service has a down-to-nothing experience. It is a time when all hell has broken loose in your life; and God has permitted the devil's hold on your soul. Intuitively, you know you are caught in a net. You cannot cut him loose, and he will not let you go. Nevertheless, each detail of every test, trial and temptation is being exquisitely executed, orchestrated and engineered by God. He reaches out over people and conditions, controlling the circumstances and protecting your interests with appointed skill, consummate care and concern.

Whether you're reading this book in the privacy of your home, a public park, a palace veranda, a political cloak room or a prison cell, the message of your down-to-nothing time is still the same. It is the message that there is no substitute for Christ. He is the answer to your every question and the solution to your every problem. He, and He alone, has divinely designed the circumstantial center and circumference of your life for His ultimate glory and your ultimate good. All of your mistakes and failures have been factored into creation of the divine masterpiece that is you. No one and nothing can touch you without His permission.

A down-to-nothing time is the most precious and valuable time of your life. It is a time that has been lovingly planned by God to develop you into the masterpiece of the man or woman that He created you to be. When you are able to see your down-to-nothing time as the potter's wheel, God as the Master Potter, and you as the servant clay, God shall then be able to mold and make you, and put you on display, as a "trophy of His grace."

In her classic autobiography, *My Life With Martin Luther King, Jr.*, the late Coretta Scott King, shares with her readers that, on the day of their wedding, and a short while before the actual wedding ceremony, Daddy King, Martin Luther King, Jr.'s father, took her and Martin aside for the little talk he always gave young couples before he married them.

Daddy King said to Coretta and Martin: "Coretta, if I were you, I would not marry M.L. unless I could not help myself. M.L., I would not marry Coretta unless I could not help myself. I preach because I can't help myself, and, when you get married you should think of it like that, as something you are impelled to do."

I have written this, my first book, because I could not help myself. It is my response to the repeated call of the Holy Spirit. He has called to do a new thing in me and through me. He has called to pour me out a blessing that there will not be room enough to receive it.

Finally, in the tradition of the saints of old, I believe I'll testify while I have a chance.

January 19, 2008   Barbara Washington Franklin, Esq.
Washington, D.C.

"When You're *Down* To Nothing, God Is *Up* To Something"

What a blessing it is to realize at least five of the most precious and valuable biblical truths mastered and modeled by Jesus and given to us by the Father to light the sometimes treacherous, albeit ultimately triumphant, pathway of our Christian journey.

The first of these truths is that every life that God intends to use mightily in His service has a down-to-nothing experience. Jesus did. Saul of Tarsus did. Job did. Daniel and David did. The Israelites did. Esther did. Shadrack, Meshack and Abednego did. Joseph did. Lazarus, Mary and Martha did.

One wise soul has stated this all-important and life-changing first truth in a nutshell: "*When you're down to nothing, God is up to something.*" While the specific details of our down-to-nothing times will vary, this eternal truth will not. A down-to-nothing time is a time of pain, struggle, hardship, disappointment, trial, seemingly unanswered prayers; a time of helplessness through the loss of a job or long illness, fractured relationships or being forcibly separated from those we love.

It is a time of being at your wits' end in the face of some overwhelming circumstance. All hell breaks loose in your life and there's nothing you can do to stem the tide. Your emotions ride the roller coaster of disappointment, grief and discouragement. There's no medicine to dissolve the ache in your heart.

It is a time when some circumstance in your life has put you under tremendous pressure, has you feeling hemmed in, and perhaps even embarrassed by some public disgrace you never imagined possible. Try as you might, this is one crucible you can't escape. Intuitively, you know you're in the devil's grip; you can't shake him loose and He won't let go.

The second truth is that God is in absolute control. Whether our suffering and trial have been caused by our actions or the actions of others is not the issue. Rather, the issue is the sovereignty of God, His will, plan and purpose for our life. Critical to our spiritual maturity is the knowledge that God orchestrates and engineers our

21

circumstances right down to the smallest detail. He calls all the shots and rules and overrules in every instance.

The third truth is that no evil can touch us without God's knowledge and permission. This truth is classically illustrated in the dialogue between the Father and Satan, regarding God's servant Job. Satan had to obtain God's permission to heap suffering and hardship on Job. In the end, God restored sevenfold to Job all that he had lost. Satan had to once again be reminded that God alone is God, and he is not. We, too, must be reminded that God alone is God, and we are not.

No matter how excruciating our down-to-nothing time may be, our heavenly Father has lovingly and brilliantly designed our down-to-nothing time as a time of spiritual growth and maturation. He uses this time of testing and trial to teach us of His everlasting love; and that we can trust Him, no matter how threatening and desperate our circumstances may be. He uses it to teach us that He will never leave us and, therefore, we are never alone. He uses it to teach us that the battles we face are never ours, but His alone to fight. And lastly, He desires so much to teach us of His faithfulness when our backs are against the wall.

The fourth truth is that God wants us to use trouble as the starting point to do a new thing in our life. How precious it is to know that before trouble knocks on our door, God already has a plan by which He can bring good out of pain, suffering, hardship and trial (Romans 8:28). Whether He does or not will always depend on how we see and respond to the trouble. If we see the trouble as coming from God's hand and respond rightly, God will turn our tribulation, and even tragedy, into triumph and trophies.

The fifth and final truth is that, without our down-to-nothing time, we would not be able to handle, with gratitude, humility and grace, the cornucopia of blessings—pressed down, shaken together and running over—that God has prepared for us. When God begins to bless us going out and coming in, we are able to remain humble in the knowledge that it is God who gives us the power to harvest crops we didn't sow and inhabit houses we didn't build.

No matter how painful our tests and trials may be, nothing pleases the Father more than when we respond, at the core of our being, in complete trust and surrender to His will and purpose for our life. We take up our cross and follow Him wherever He leads. We remain calm and secure in the knowledge of Christ, our Savior. We don't become angry or depressed by the actions of others in their dealings against us.

Our Christ-colored perspective trains and disciplines us to see others as mere tools used by the Father to spiritually mature us. We allow the Father to teach us that the harsh words, evil actions and negative attitudes of others are His sandpaper, hammer and nails to smooth our rough edges and to humble, shape and sculpt us into the holy men and women fit to be called saints of God; and fit to carry out the work of the Holy Spirit in the earth.

The Father wants to give us the most precious and priceless gift that He alone can give. It is the gift of seeing, through eyes of faith, our down-to-nothing time as our opportunity to grow spiritually by leaps and bounds; and our opportunity to learn spiritual truths that will take us from here to eternity. Our down-to-nothing time is our spiritual foundation for the realization that God has gone ahead to meet us, no matter what the destination; that He has promised that He will never leave us alone; that what others mean for evil, God means for His glory and our ultimate good (Genesis 45:5-8); and that *"No weapon that is formed against thee shall prosper; and every tongue that shall rise against thee in judgment thou shalt condemn. This is the heritage of the servants of the Lord, and their righteousness is of all, saith the Lord"* (Isaiah 54:17).

Think of the needless heartache, pain and emotional turmoil that would be avoided if we knew that no matter how tough the trying time; no matter how heavy our load, we can remain calm and peaceful when under siege and satanic attack. We can forgive those who have, without cause, regret or remorse, trespassed against us — sometimes brutally so. We can count it all joy when we are faced with temptations and difficulties beyond what we think we can bear (James: 1:2).

The next time you arrive at your down-to-nothing time, see God as up to accomplishing something fantastic, and so far beyond your wildest imagination and fondest dreams. Your job is to remain stead-fast, head up, back straight, hands to the plow, and your spirit determined to keep your eyes on Jesus, in victorious praise and adoration to the Father, for having already done what He said He would do.

God Is In Charge

At all times and in all places, God is in charge. In good times and in bad times, God is in charge. In sunshine and in rain, God is in charge. In the center of the tsunami and at the heart of the hurricane, God is in charge. When the storms of life batter and bruise us badly, God is in charge.

When I have been wronged by others or when I have wronged another, God is in charge. When I have been falsely accused or when I have falsely accused, God is in charge. When we have been denied the justice due us, God is in charge. When others take advantage of us, God is in charge. When those we love the most, hurt us the deepest, God is in charge. When all hell breaks loose in our life, God is in charge. When Satan seems to have trumped the Savior, God is in charge. When the wicked confidently command the arena and the righteous fearfully sit on the sidelines, God is in charge.

When loyalty is laughed at and treachery is touted, God is in charge. When your best friend becomes your worst enemy, God is in charge. When the world takes center stage in your life, and Jesus is relegated to the balcony, God is in charge. When our "struggles have struggles," God is in charge. When our mountains won't move an inch, God is in charge.

When Goliath seems to be taking steroids, God is in charge. When the Red Sea is a breath away, and the Egyptians are at our heels, God is in charge. When your doctor suggests you get your affairs in order, God is in charge. When disappointment couldn't enter your front door, but now knocks on your back door, God is in charge. When discouragement is in your cup of coffee and despair is on every page of your morning newspaper, God is in charge.

When I was growing up, we used to sing a favorite church song in Sunday school and in Sunday morning service. It included the lyrics: "*It is no secret what God can do. What He's done for others, He'll do for you.*" No matter what you've been through, what you're going through, what's being done to you, said about you or taken from you, God is still in charge. Whatever *has* happened or is *now* happening in your life, your circumstance has been caused by one of three sources: either God has caused it, or He has allowed Satan to cause it, or He has allowed you to cause it.

Nevertheless, we can take heart and thank and praise God for our circumstance, no matter how difficult it may be. This is because *"And we know that all things work together for good to them that love God, to them who are the called according to His purpose"* (Romans 8:28). This foundational biblical promise allows us to know that no evil tiding can ever trump the plan and purpose of God for our life. We have been bought with a price and are safe in His arms for all eternity (I Corinthians 6:20); because God is in charge.

"Do Whatever He Tells You"

One of my favorite Bible stories is that of the wedding in the Village of Cana in Galilee. The wedding reception was in full swing, when the bride and groom were informed that they had run out of wine.

To respectfully paraphrase Scripture, I imagine Mary, the mother of Jesus, was informed of the dilemma. She was asked if she would enlist Jesus' help. As any proud mother of a celebrity son, Mary said certainly Jesus would help. But there was just one condition that must first be met. "And what is that?" they probably inquired. "*Do whatever He tells you,*" instructed Mary (John 2:5 NIV).

Mary knew that her son was no ordinary guest in attendance. She also knew that Jesus was famous for His unorthodox formulas for solving the myriad of problems facing the people of His day.

I can imagine the expression on the faces of those Jesus told to fill the empty wine jars with water. I am sure others whispered in the background, "When did water take the place of more wine?" Nevertheless, having been admonished by Mary, the catering staff followed Jesus' instructions to the letter. And in the twinkling of an eye, the water became wine. The specific prayer request was answered.

I wonder what my reaction would have been if I had been there. Would I have dared question Mary, having heard so much about Jesus? Would I have had the faith to believe Jesus? Or would I have had the temerity to second-guess the Son of God?

During times without number, the voice of the Holy Spirit, speaking through Mary, has whispered in our ears. It characteristically tells us to, "*Do whatever He tells you.*" We hesitate, procrastinate and pontificate. We just will not obey the voice of God. Or to paraphrase the words of Oswald Chambers, "*the problem with most of us is simply that we won't.*"

Our bottles are empty and we need a new supply. But we refuse to do what we have been told by the Holy Spirit to do. Consequently, our deepest prayers go unanswered. Our deepest desires remain unfulfilled. Our doubt keeps us without.

We would rather do what our mothers tell us; what our best friend tells us; what our mentor tells us; what our spiritual advisor tells us; what the boss tells us; what the psychic tells us; what the doctor tells us; what the lawyer tells us; what our frat brother tells us; what our co-worker tells us; what our club member tells us; and what any and everybody else tells us.

After all, what can the Maker of the Universe tell us that our contemporaries can't tell us? We keep marvelous and magnificent blessings of God meant just for us on hold, by failing and refusing to do whatever He tells us.

"Faith Is the Refusal to Panic"

In 2 Timothy 1:7, Paul tells us: *"For God hath not given us the spirit of fear; but of power, and of love, and of a sound mind."*

I have discovered Satan's most effective weapon in his demonic arsenal used to defeat the children of God. It is the creation of circumstances in our lives that cause us to panic. We commonly refer to our reactions to these times as panic attacks.

Most of us, at one time or another, have experienced a panic attack. The cause of the attack can originate with a message left at our home or office; a piece of mail slipped in the mail slot of the front door; or a call from the hospital saying we need a follow up mammogram to the one we just took a few days ago.

We feel threatened. We feel exposed. We feel vulnerable. We feel scared. We feel attacked. We panic. Our chest tightens. Our muscles stiffen. Our breathing becomes labored. Our teeth are set on edge.

Why such emotional and physical reaction? Primarily it's because whatever we perceive as threatening, we also perceive ourselves as standing alone in the midst of the attack. This faulty perception causes us to panic. While under attack, we see ourselves as helpless. In this regard, we see ourselves rightly. Human beings and helplessness go together as coffee and cream and as eggs and bacon.

As believers, we are always being challenged to look up and see Jesus standing by. Depending on what the situation calls for in terms of our peace, protection, power, and prosperity, He will be standing on either side of us, in front of us or in back of us. It's up to us to see Him. And in the words of Dr. Martyn Lloyd-Jones, *"Faith is the refusal to panic."*

Jesus has promised us in his Word that He will never leave us nor forsake us. Never means never.

Shadrach, Meshak and Abednego can testify that while Jesus may not keep you out of your furnace, He'll walk around in the midst of the flames with you. And when you come out of the furnace, not even the smell of smoke will be on you; not one strand of hair will have been singed; and you'll be free of the shackles that had you bound. Daniel 3:25.

Esther can testify that while you may have to go alone to the King, and prepared to risk perishing, if necessary, the Holy Spirit will give you the exact words to plead your case and prevail against the Namans of this world. Esther 7:3-4.

David, if called on, would testify that even if you have only limited resources at your disposal, such as a sling shot and stones to war against the Giant in your life, God can and will give you the victory, if you stand and allow Him to fight your battle, knowing in the deepest part of your spirit that the battle is not yours, but the Lord's. I Samuel 17:49-50.

Abraham and Sarah, if called on, would testify that God is able. He doesn't need our help. If He makes us a promise, He is able to fulfill it. Genesis 21:2-3. It is our job to remember that *"His ways are not our ways"* and His timing is above and beyond our comprehension.

These are just a few of the biblical heroes and heroines of faith that serve to remind us that we need not panic if we keep our focus on Jesus and not what usually turns out to be the smoke and mirrors put before us by those who walk in darkness.

There have been countless times when I responded to evil tidings in panic. Nevertheless, I was determined to keep my eyes on Jesus. I would keep on keeping on. I would never give up. *I would persist past the point of pain.* I would persevere through the sunshine and the rain. *I would trust God, and trust God, and trust God.*

When hit from the blind side, as Disciples of Christ Jesus, we must resolve to refuse to panic. Moreover, having been washed in the blood of Jesus, we must remain calm when all Hell is breaking loose around us. God will honor your faith by ushering in His angels all around you to protect and keep you from even *"dashing your foot against a stone,"* (Psalm 91:12) and ever make ready your circumstances for the victory that is already yours.

As believers, we have been endowed and imbued with the capacity to walk on water when Jesus says "Come." All of us at one time or another have managed to summon the will to get out of the boat. We are shocked that we are, in fact, walking on water towards Jesus. We have responded to the whispers of heaven, and are spiritually attuned to the call of the Master. We have wisely left the management of the winds and waves to Him.

One day, you'll realize that the power and peace of God so protects you from panic, that you have become impervious to panic through the power of the Holy Spirit resident within you.

"Relentlessly Keep Your Word"

Nothing moves the hand of God more than our faithful and bold commitment to relentlessly keep our word.

I once watched a cable television show in which a select panel of speakers addressed various topics in their advice and counsel to new Members of Congress. I shall always remember one speaker's cogent, yet critical, advice to these Freshman Members: "Relentlessly keep your word." The speaker went on to say that relentlessly keeping their word to their colleagues would sometimes cost them dearly. However, ultimately, they would pay a much higher price for not keeping their word. For sooner or later, it would be the word of their colleague that they would depend on to meet a constituent need or fulfill a constituent promise.

Having worked on Capitol Hill during the Carter Administration as the Minority (Republican) Chief Counsel and Staff Director to the late Congressman Stewart B. McKinney (R-CT), the then Ranking Member of the House Committee on the District of Columbia, I can easily verify that relentlessly keeping your word is the implicit code of honor on Capitol Hill. Put simply, this is how the Hill works. But the importance of relentlessly keeping your word is not confined to the Hill. It is how life, in general, works. Life, in general, is about relationships; and relationships are about relentlessly keeping your word—or they should be.

Keeping your word relentlessly is the first rule of love as taught by Jesus Christ. What, above all, characterizes our relationship with God the Father, God the Son and God the Holy Ghost? It is the Word of God. In the twenty-fourth chapter of the Gospel of Matthew, the thirty-fifth verse, Jesus tells us that "...*Heaven and earth shall pass away, but my word shall never pass away.*"

As Disciples of Christ, we know the power of the Word of God. God's Word heals, saves, provides, protects, shields, restores, empowers, discerns, makes wise, and perceives. Generation, after generation, of Christian believers testifies to the presence and power of the Word of God.

There was a time in our culture when a man's word and hand-shake was all that was needed to seal a deal of any kind. Today, we are so accustomed to hearing untruth and partial truths, if someone says let's meet on Friday, we are tempted to ask for a written contract. Too frequently, our word just doesn't mean anything anymore. And when it does, people are often astonished.

Once you have experienced the loss of loved ones, the value and importance of our words is magnified. For it is the word of our departed loved ones that we remember most and deeply cherish. We realize that we keep our loved one's words in our hearts and in our minds. We don't need a storage bin, file cabinets, or CD-ROMs to keep them. We just keep them in our hearts where no one can take them from us or even see them.

Did not Jesus tell us, "*...If you love me, keep my command-ments*" (John 14:15). *"For they are life and healing to your souls."* In other words, keep my words and live. And in the Book of Joshua, God told Joshua *"This book of the law shall not depart out of thy mouth; but thou shalt meditate therein day and night, that thou mayest observe to do according to all that is written therein, for then thou shalt make thy way prosperous, and then thou shalt have good success"* (Joshua 1:8). Long before the panel of speakers advised the new Members of Congress, God had already given them the same advice long before they became new members, and long before the Congress was envisioned and later established.

"This Thing Is From Me"

I could have entitled this essay "In every detail, God is in control." In fact, initially, I had done just that until a close friend, and sister-in-Christ, gave me, as a birthday gift, a copy of L.B. (Mrs. Charles E.) Cowman's classic *Streams in the Desert* (Zondervan: Grand Rapids, MI, 1997). It is a book of 366 devotional readings—one for each day of the year. The author expertly threads and mightily heralds, from cover to cover, the central message of the Gospel which is that Jesus is "*...the way, the truth and the life...*" and that no man cometh unto the Father but by Him (John 14:6).

Not only have I been encouraged and inspired by each of the readings, but this entire work has deeply impacted my Christian walk. I have also been led to incorporate, throughout this collection, a number of the author's unique expressions of certain biblical principles that I consider powerful and persuasive. I shall always be grateful to the Holy Spirit for prompting my sister-friend to put L.B. Cowman's outstanding work in my hands at the appointed time.

However, the devotional that masterfully confirmed for me what God had been speaking to my heart in recent years is simply captioned, "February 1." This reading is introduced with a citation of 1 Kings 12:24 (NIV) which consists of a mere four words: "*This is my doing*" (Op. Cit., p. 56). Cowman persuades the reader that no matter what he or she might be going through, it is the Lord's doing.

This scripture is also eloquently expressed in the King James Version when it states: "*This thing is from Me.*" No matter what you might be going through, it is the Lord's doing. In every circumstance, and in every detail, God is whispering, "*This thing is from Me.*" You are having trouble making ends meet financially. "*This thing is from Me.*" *I want to teach you to look to me for your supply.* Your spouse has been unfaithful. "*This thing is from Me.*" *I want to teach you that whoever has offended you has offended me even greater. If I can forgive the greater offence, why can't you forgive the lesser offense?*"

34

The enemy comes in like a flood. *"This thing is from Me."* I want *to convince you that you are never alone. I am with you no matter how serious your situation may be. I want to teach you that you and I are a majority. I want to teach you that if you follow My orders, when you come out of the fire, not even the smell of smoke will be on your clothes. I want to teach you that when you let Me go before you in battle, you shall come out more than a conqueror through Him who loved you.*

You are so weary and worn from the battle. *"This thing is from Me."* I want you to master the lesson that the battle is not yours, but mine. All you have to do is show up for the fight, and let me take the blows. The storm never seems to end. "This thing is from Me." The storm will end when my plan and purpose for the storm has been accomplished and not one minute sooner.*

Through one illustration after another, Cowman convinces her readers that no matter what we might be going through, if we will have faith in God's word that tells us that *"This thing is from Me,"* the storm clouds that may rise and dark winds that may blow "will soon pass over and the sun will shine in all of its splendor."

Straw Hat Warriors

The two women who have had the most significant impact on my life that shall last for all eternity have been my mother, Eunice Vetta Ross Washington, ("Mother") and my paternal grandmother, Rosa Lee Bradley Washington Terry ("Mama"). They have had the greatest impact because they not only *talked* the Christian talk, they *walked* the Christian walk before us day-in-and-day-out; in sunshine and in rain; in good times and in bad times.

Mother and Mama remained steadfast, no matter how threatening the storm, or how severe the raging waters, or fierce winds they had to face. Years later, as an adult, when I looked back on my childhood, I came to realize that, in response to the carnal weapons that were inevitably formed against them as they proceeded on their Christian journey, they, in faith, chose as their armor their prayers and songs of praise and deliverance to the Almighty God.

When the work week and school week were over, we knew that the next major event to round out the previous week and get us ready for the week ahead was our attendance at church *and* Sunday school on Sunday morning. Attendance at church and Sunday school was as mandatory as regular school attendance. Mama and Mother's attitude, reflected in all their actions, was that of Joshua when he said, "*...choose ye this day whom ye will serve...but as for me and my house, we shall serve the Lord*" (Joshua 24:15).

No matter what problems confronted them, Mother and Mama faced them head on. Or should I say hat on, because neither considered herself fully dressed for Sunday service until she had donned her latest wide brimmed straw hat in the Spring and Summer; and felt and wool hats just as wide in the Fall and Winter. With regard to their hats, they adopted as their theme the slogan of the noted milliner and fashion designer, the late Emily Miles, whose slogan was, "Above all, the right hat." Their total outfits matched to a tee. They were "*fashionistas with flair.*" Every time I looked at Mother or Mama walk out the front door, their heads held high and their shoulders back, their appearance said unequivocally, "I know who I am and I know Whose I am. Make no mistake about it."

Mama and Mother, almost exclusively by example, taught us that when faced with a difficult situation, a particular hardship or a trial of some kind that might even amount to a public disgrace; the first thing you must do is to go to the Lord in prayer. And at the throne of grace, pour out to Him the trouble you face and ask Him to help you.

I always knew when Mother or Mama was burdened with one problem or another. They didn't complain, blame, fuss, moan or groan. Instead, while standing at the kitchen sink washing dishes, or while in the bedroom making up beds, or while standing in front of the stove cooking collard greens and cornbread, they would enthusiastically sing their favorite lyrics from church hymns and gospel songs.

Some of these lyrics, so very familiar to me, would include: "*Ask the Savior to help you, comfort, strengthen and keep you...Sweet hour of prayer, sweet hour of prayer, that calls me from a world of care, and bids me at my Father's throne, make all my wants and wishes known...Nearer, my God to Thee, nearer to Thee. E'en though it be a cross that raiseth me...He's sweet, I know; He's sweet, I know. Storm clouds may rise; strong winds may blow. I'll tell the world, wherever I go, that I've found a Savior, and He's sweet, I know.*"

Mother and Mama reverenced their God and respected themselves. They knew who they were and whose they were. The very cells of their skin exuded their spirit of a conqueror. In fact, they regarded themselves as *more than conquerors, more than over comers and more than victors.* They didn't complain. They didn't murmur. They didn't doubt. They talked like warriors. They thought like warriors. They behaved like warriors. And when necessary, they spoke truth to power like warriors. The fact that their helmets were straw hats didn't dilute their prevailing power as warriors. They could have left no greater legacy to their children and their children's children.

Thank you, Mother and Mama.

Revenge Can't Win. What You Send Returns Again.

Nothing wastes more precious time than the preoccupation of getting even. Spending time getting back at someone that you consider to have hurt you in some way is the preeminent time waster. Moreover, we shall never be able to fulfill our divine destiny if we spend precious time engaged in getting back at others. When we are spiritually wise, we realize that we are trying to do what is humanly impossible.

Revenge does not work because what we send out comes back. What we sow, we reap. The evil we send out inevitably comes back to our door multiplied again, and again, and again. The evil we sow, albeit the size of a mustard seed, takes root and sprouts all over our life and affairs, and spills over into the life and affairs of others in our midst.

God does not want us to contaminate our souls with the spirit of revenge. He says to us, "...*Dearly beloved, avenge not yourselves... for it is written, vengeance is mine; I will repay, saith the Lord*" (Romans 12:19). He doesn't say how and He doesn't say when. But we know that He is a Man that does not lie. We also know that we can trust the Man who died for us.

God has told us that it is His job to settle scores, pay back and take vengeance. Therefore, when we engage in the business of getting even, for any reason, we are attempting to invade the domain of the Most High. We shall never be able to pre-empt God in any sphere of life. And that includes the area of revenge. The sooner we stop playing Jesus, Jr., the better for us and all concerned.

With regard to getting even, the Holy Spirit would have us follow the admonition of the apostle Paul found in Romans 12:14: "...*Bless them which persecute you; bless, and curse not.*"

You Are Perfect For Your Purpose

The way you smile when you're pleased; your taste for rum raisin ice cream; your desire for order in your surroundings; your need for tranquility and solitude; your love of books and libraries; your penchant for fast cars and pretty women; your charisma that draws friends and foes alike; your love of Chopin and Jazz concerts in the park; the way you wear your hair and clothes; your faith that shakes, but still bakes—all these attributes make you perfect for your divine purpose. In the words of one unknown author:

> "You're a person who's uniquely
> and wonderfully made.
> You're a masterpiece of creativity,
> a one-of-a-kind original,
> an amazing miracle,
> handcrafted by God Himself.
>
> Distinctive, exceptional, exclusive,
> extraordinary, incomparable, individual,
> original, rare, unequalled.
>
> See yourself the way He sees you,
> as an incredibly special person
> with unique and wonderful gifts
> to share with our world."

See yourself from the Divine perspective: a child of God. Therefore, you're a visionary, trendsetter and maverick; incredibly capable of blessing our world through the sacred use of your God-given gifts and talents. See yourself as proof positive that "*He performs wonders that cannot be fathomed, miracles that cannot be counted*" (Job 9:10 NIV). Yes, you are fearfully, wonderfully and miraculously made.

Everything you need to fulfill your divine assignment has already been given to you. God has blessed you with every spiritual blessing. Your unique gifts, skills and talents bestowed upon you by the Father make you perfect for your purpose. Your challenge is to recognize your talents and then spiritually discern how God wants you to use them to bless your fellow man, and in so doing, contribute to the uplift and healing of the nations.

The time of your birth; the identity and ethnic background of your parents; whether you're male or female; the shape of your body; the color of your skin — everyone of these factors has been determined by God long before you were shaped in your mother's womb.

God has seen to it that you are perfect for your purpose. In Matthew 10:30 we are reminded, *"But the very hairs of your head are all numbered."* God does not make any mistakes. He knows exactly what personal attributes you will need to carry out his will for your life and to fulfill your mission in the world.

It does nothing less than grieves the heart of God to have you complain about the circumstances of your birth; the color of your skin; the ethnic and educational background of your parents; the limited opportunities of your childhood; and the overall mistreatment that you were subjected to by family members and others.

When you board the complaint train in any direction, just remember that God knows exactly what He's doing, and it doesn't pay to second guess Him. He didn't consult you when He created the universe. And He doesn't find it necessary to check in with you to keep it going.

When we are questioning who we are not, what we don't have and what we can't do, it is usually because we are remiss in making it a priority to schedule daily quality time to pray, read and meditate on the Word of God.

In addition, we are carrying out an assignment that God never intended for us, but for another. We are walking in someone else's shoes, wearing someone else's hat, and driving someone else's car. In other words, we are playing the role and acting the part that God never meant for us to play or to act. It is the role and part that is to be played by another. And so it is no wonder that "our eyes are dead and we are dead behind them."

In our willful refusal to answer God's call on our life, however foolish His call may appear to the world, we are telling God that we choose disobedience to His will over surrender to His divine plan and purpose. We are telling God that His unconditional love for us is not unconditional enough.

Almost without exception, when your work matches your passions, you can be certain that you have discovered God's will for your life; that you are perfect for your purpose; and are living according to God's eternal plan for your life. After you've done all you can, you must just stand and adopt as your personal motto that of Quincy Jones: "Accept your creativity with humility and your success with grace."

"Go Through Hell And Make It Pay"

During my law school years, I became an avid reader of the writings of Catherine Ponder, the noted author, lecturer and ordained minister of the non-denominational Unity faith. I literally devoured, from cover to cover, the spiritual principles taught in her classic work, *The Dynamic Laws of Prosperity* (Prentice-Hall, Inc.: Englewood Cliffs, New Jersey, 1962, p. 113). My study and practical application of these spiritual principles helped to sustain me during some of the most difficult times of my life.

I also began to learn the spiritual wisdom and immeasurable wealth of seeing a particular hardship, difficulty or trial from God's perspective. In her discussion of making the most of your present situation, and not feeling "trapped" by present conditions, she instructs the reader, albeit through the words of one of her friends, "When you go through hell, make it pay—with greater understanding than you previously had, and the result of good from that experience will be lasting." (Op. Cit., p. 113). The spiritual purpose of hardship, pain and trial is designed by the Almighty to impart into his beloved children the spiritual attributes of faith, strength, wisdom, courage, confidence, conviction, resilience, vision and iron will needed to manage the vicissitudes of life, as well as handle life as a Christian in the land of milk and honey.

In other words, when you find yourself in the throes of difficult situations, a hardship of any kind, intense pressure of one sort or another, trials on every side, temptations on every hand, real painful stuff by anyone's definition, stop and thank God that He has loved you too much to leave you as you are. Therefore, He intentionally allows you to be sifted by circumstances beyond your control for the express purpose of spiritually maturing you; for molding you into an iron saint; for conforming you to the image of His Dear Son.

You now have the opportunity to be compensated by the experience in coins of increased wisdom, physical strength, emotional stamina, mental acumen, deeper intuition and the spiritual insight to see beyond what is showing. When you are released from a hellish experience, you will come out blessed by it and bold enough to be a blessing to others because of it. David tells us in Psalm 66:12, *"Thou hast caused men to ride over our heads; we went through fire and through water; but thou broughtest us out into a wealthy place."* In other words, there is immeasurable wealth in hardship, trial and tribulation.

No experience leaves us where it finds us. Hellish experiences are guaranteed to leave us either bitter or better. As someone has said, "It's a matter of one letter." Will you stop at "e" or emotionally continue on down the alphabet road to "i"? It's always your choice. *"And if it seem evil unto you to serve the Lord, choose you this day whom ye will serve; whether the gods which your fathers served that were on the other side of the flood or the gods of the Amorites in whose land ye dwell; but as for me and my house, we will serve the Lord"* (Joshua 24:15). As humans, we must all endure conditions that have the potential to crush us in defeat or to catapult us into a cornucopia of blessings with our name on it.

Pain is designed to train. That is all. Our pain comes to pass. When we see Jesus at the center of our crucible, no matter how crushing the experience, our pain must pass. Stand the test and take God's best. Recognize the experience, however painful, as a mere teaching moment against the backdrop of eternity. A moment created before the beginning of time for the salvation of our soul and its endurance throughout eternity.

"Hellish Circumstances Confirm the Importance of Your Assignment"

"Hellish circumstances confirm the importance of your assignment," instructs Dr. Mike Murdock. In Mel Gibson's unorthodox movie presentation *The Passion of the Christ*, one scene will always be embedded in my mind and memory. It is the scene of Jesus in the Garden of Gethsemane, prostrate on the ground before the Father. Jesus slowly raises His head and sees Satan standing a few feet away from Him.

Satan has a smirk on his face. He is happy, even gleeful, at Jesus' predicament. Jesus is alone, suffering, abandoned, but nevertheless, pleading with the Father, "*O my Father, if it be possible, let this cup pass from me; nevertheless, not as I will, but as thou wilt*" (Matthew 26:39).

Satan is jumping-up-and-down happy. Jesus couldn't be in a worse situation— humanly speaking, that is. But where is His Father? I imagine Satan saying to himself, "I thought His Father was always sitting on ready, willing and able to help His Son in a jam. Clearly this is not happening at Gethsemane. Is the Father taking a time-out and didn't bother to tell Jesus?"

Like Jesus, when we find ourselves in the deepest of hellish circumstances that we could ever imagine, Satan draws nigh. And, for a brief moment or split second, Satan might get our attention. But in the Garden of Gethsemane, Jesus teaches us what must be the believers' stance when faced with hellish circumstances. Jesus was able to look beyond Satan and his hellish circumstance of the moment and remember His Father's absolute sovereignty in the world.

Jesus also recalled His sonship with the Father. Jesus was so spiritually aligned with the Father, that after asking His Father to let the bitter cup of His impending crucifixion pass, He quickly yielded. Jesus surrendered to the divine plan and purpose for His life. This is evident when Jesus prayed, "*...nevertheless, not as I will, but as thou wilt*" (Matthew 26:3).

Jesus knew that the assignment of the Cross was the centerpiece of His mission as Savior of mankind. In His obedience to the Father, Jesus made no attempt to escape the divine crucible. We, like Jesus, have a cross that awaits us. It might be either a time of deep pain and suffering, the loss of a loved one, some form of humiliation, or even a public disgrace that we could never have imagined we would have to experience. Nevertheless, it is important to remember that our cross is the centerpiece of our divine assignment. Of this I am sure, because of the unconditional love of Jesus.

During these most difficult times, we must, nevertheless, take heart because Heaven is in view. And it is the Heavenly Father that is controlling the deepest of our hellish circumstances. Jesus never forgot this truth. Jesus challenges us to remember that no matter how excruciating the particular pain of our present condition, God is still in charge. He is above man. He is ruling and overruling at every moment, every hour, and every day.

Satan draws nigh in the midst of our hellish circumstances. He would have given anything to have Jesus, while in the garden, curse God and die. But Jesus knew that He was nearing the completion of His assignment. His great reward of the resurrection was just around the corner. Knowing this, Jesus refused to give up, give in or give out. He decided to hang tough. But for His implacable stance, we would not be here today to talk about it.

Emerson said that *"Prayer is the contemplation of the facts of life from the highest point of view."*

The facts of life include the hellish circumstances that surround us. Given that the Father is engineering our circumstances, hellish circumstances should really be a time of great rejoicing. It should be a time of recognizing that God is never closer to us than He is when, intuitively, we know that we are caught in Satan's grip. Satan's focus and concentration on us is an indication of just how important our assignment is in the overall plan and purpose of God. Significantly, "hellish circumstances confirm the importance of your assignment."

Hellish circumstances can also be a barometer to the resurrected life that awaits us. Our responsibility is to be willing to surrender to the cross that awaits us. We must refrain from shutting down, packing up, quitting and running. That is the way of the unbeliever when the heat is turned up. Whereas an attitude of surrender says, "Your will, Your way, Your time, Lord." The prayer of surrender says, "Thy will be done."

We then allow the Holy Spirit to select the nails that will pierce our hands and feet. We allow God to determine the manner in which the stone in front of our tomb is rolled away. And finally, we get ready for Easter morning, the dawn of a new day, and our resurrection to a new and glorious life in Christ Jesus.

One day we shall look back and realize that our journey to Calvary was worth every jagged road, crooked path, uphill climb, deep water, fiery furnace and rugged terrain that we had to endure. The Grand Architect of the universe knew what He was doing after all.

"The Tragedy Is Not Unanswered Prayer, But Unoffered Prayer"

At one time or another, we all experience the tragedy of unanswered prayer. But how much more satisfying, rewarding and joyous our lives would be if we'd view unanswered prayer from the perspective of author L.B. Cowman who wisely counseled her readers that "The tragedy is not unanswered prayer, but unoffered prayer."

How many times have you urgently needed material supply, in one form or another? At the moment, perhaps what's most needed is a parking space, money to pay a bill, the healing of your sick body, the readjustment of a relationship, the establishment of peace and harmony in your home or office, a job, adequate housing for your family, a car note, your children's tuition, or the repayment of a long overdue personal loan.

How many times, in prayer, have you asked God to supply your need? Why have you not brought your request to the throne of grace? Is there a need that you believe that is above and beyond the reach of prayer? Do you consider your needs to be unimportant to the Father, because they are insignificant to others? Is there anything too hard for God? Or are you simply perishing, even at this late date, from the lack of knowledge given to us by L.B. Cowman when she states: "...*Nothing lies beyond the reach of prayer except those things outside the will of God...When genuine prayer is even whispered, earth and heaven, and the past and future, say, 'Amen!'*" (Op. Cit., p. 250).

Have you not been told that "*There is no secret what God can do. What He's done for others, He'll do for you.*" However, there are certain things that He won't do for us until we ask Him to help us. Dr. Charles Stanly expresses it this way: "*God is just sitting on ready, waiting for you to come to Him with your prayer requests.*" The fact that God sits ready and waiting for me to come to Him with my prayer requests is sometimes more than I can bear. Admittedly, my finite mind, with all the faith I can muster, still, on occasion, wrestles with this knowledge of the goodness and mercy of the Lord, as it pertains to my provision, protection and peace.

According to the late Rev. Dr. Kenneth E. Hagin, God has told us in His Word that "...He is *El Shaddai* — the God Who is more than enough!" Moreover, Dr. Hagin states that the literal Greek translation of John 14:13 says: *"If you will ask anything in My Name, if I don't have it, I'll make if for you!"* (*El Shaddai*, RHEMA Bible Church: Tulsa, OK, 1985, p. 10).

Have you been too busy to pray? In his wonderfully refreshing work, *Too Busy Not To Pray*, (Inter Varsity Press: Downers Grove, IL, 1998), Pastor Bill Hybels, faithfully admonishes us: "We should be too busy *not* to pray." Nothing makes more of a difference in your life than to examine the circumstances in your life that you consider pressing or even tragic, and ask yourself, "When was the last time I sought the Lord in fervent prayer for the solution to my problem?"

Turn Your Back To The Lions

Nothing is more effective to achieving the right resolution of a great problem or trouble that has come into your life than to literally and figuratively turn your back to it.

To do so is not to deny the problem, as it were, but to demonstrate the level of your faith in an Almighty God who has promised, over and over again in His Word, to protect you from every kind and kin of lions either stalking your path or staring you down after you have been thrown into their den.

One of my favorite Bible stories is the story of Daniel in the Lions' Den. Spiritually, the story of Daniel is the story of every man, woman and child. In his classic work, *Power Through Constructive Thinking,* Dr. Emmett Fox masterfully teaches us that *"When some great problem or trouble comes into your life, you are, figuratively speaking, thrown into a pit of lions."*

In reading numerous Bibles over the years, I've always been intrigued and inspired with the pictorial description of Daniel found in some. There Daniel sits or stands, not looking at the lions, but turning his back on them; looking instead up towards heaven, looking towards Jerusalem, looking towards the light.

The lions, instead of snarling or looking angry or ferocious, are calm and peaceful as they stroll about, rest or stand with fixed gaze on Daniel — puzzled and amazed that he has turned his back to them and their very real power and ability to tear him to shreds in an instant. Moreover, the lions outnumber Daniel who has no visible means of defense.

It is the fear and trepidation that rises within us that causes the lions to roar and carry on so. Or as Florence Scovel Shinn has said in her classic work, *The Game of Life*, "The lion takes his fierceness from your fear. Walk up to the lion, and he will disappear; run away and he runs after you." (DeVorss & Company: Marina del Ray, CA, 1925, p. 54).

And in *The Power of the Spoken Word*, Shinn again instructs the reader: "The lion draws his fierceness from your fear; his roar is in the tremors of your heart. Stand still like Daniel, and you too

49

shall hear the rush of angels sent to take your part...Immediately walk up to the situation of which you are afraid. If you run away from it, it will always be right at your heels...That means not to run away from the situation, walk up fearlessly and face the lion on your pathway, and the lion turns into an airdale. The lion takes his fierceness from your fear." (DeVorss & Company: Marina del Ray, CA, 1925, pp. 27, 67-68).

Daniel's turning his back to the lions showed that he was not afraid of the lions' abilities to tear him to shreds and eat him alive. His faith in his God to save him—no matter how threatening or desperate the situation—overcame his fear. God responded to Daniel's faith by sending His angels to shut the lions' mouths.

In 1 Samuel 17:34 (NIV), we find these words: *And there came a lion.* It would appear to take a radical transformation of one's thinking and courageous action if we are to turn our back to the lions that are guaranteed to appear on the path that makes up our Christian journey.

This is because most of us are bereft of a spiritual perspective that allows us to recognize the lions, first and foremost, as "special blessings from the Lord" that have been prepared by God with consummate care and skill; and not as a cause for fear and anxiety. If we see and receive the lions as "God's opportunities in disguise," we are assured of divine, angelic protection and deliverance no matter how threatening and dangerous the situation (*see* Cowman, Op. Cit., p. 86).

If you are to live passionately for Christ, you must resolve to become a master of the art of *"turning your back to the lions."* When you find yourself overwhelmed by the sheer magnitude of the lions of problems, tests or trials—*turn your back to the lions.* When you are being stalked by the lions of fear and intimidation, anxiety and stress—*turn your back to the lions.* When the lions of lack and limitation; sickness and disease have you hemmed in without any discernable means of escape—*turn your back to these lions.* When your difficulties, trials and tests have you anxious, afraid, and intimidated— *turn your back to these lions.*

When your refusal to deny Christ in some area of your life has put you in the lions' den and at your wits' end—*turn your back to these lions.* When the lions of financial setbacks and reversals have overwhelmed you—*turn your back to these lions.* When the lions of injustice relentlessly pursue you—*turn your back to these lions.* When unexpected job layoffs and employment discrimination tag you—*turn your back to these lions.*

We turn our backs to the lions by keeping our focus on Jesus, and letting Him take care of the situation. We turn our backs to the lions by fervently praying to the Father night and day for His right resolution of the big problem or big trouble that we encounter. You notice I did not say the problem that you face, because Daniel teaches us that, initially, our proper stance in the midst of our problems should not be that of facing our problems or of staring at our problems. Our proper stance must be one of looking up to the Almighty God for His guidance and direction as to what steps must be taken that have been divinely designed to address and resolve the problem.

How, pray tell, do we turn our backs to the lions when it is our desire to live the life more abundantly; and to experience the love, peace, joy, health, wealth and self-expression that is our inheritance from the Father? We begin by knowing that every lion that has ever crossed our path, snarled at us, taken the liberty to enter our premises and turn our home upside down, has been permitted to do so by the sovereign authority of the Holy Ghost.

When we summon the courage and fortitude to turn our back to the lions, we say to the world, *"Satan, take your best shot because 'no weapon formed against me shall prosper, every tongue raised against me in judgment shall be condemned... God has not given me a spirit of fear, but of power and of love and of a sound mind...I am more than a conqueror through Him who loved me... God is my refuge and strength, a very present help in trouble... the angels of the Lord encampeth around those who fear Him and He delivereth them.'"*

The story of Daniel in the Lions' Den is, above all, an illustration of the power of prayer in the life of the individual who puts his or her faith in the presence and power of the living God to save us whether we have been ushered into the palace and surrounded by praise; or thrown into the lions' den as punishment for our practice of serving none other than the living God.

Letting Go Is The Ultimate Skill

Throughout our lifetime, we are consciously, or unconsciously, in some form or other, engaged in the process of acquiring new and additional skills. However, the foundational skill, or for purposes of this writing, the ultimate skill to which all other skills resonate and respond, is the skill of letting go.

What trips most of us up on the path of achieving a good success in life is our reluctance, if not outright refusal, to let go of that which, by divine design, has completed its purpose according to God's will and plan for our life. The "that" referred to comes in innumerable forms and all the endless, myriad things we sort, file, box, pack, store, ship and insure. Some of these "things" that we clutch and hang onto long after they are meant to be released are quite familiar, and to name a few, include the following: relationships, clothes, personal papers, business files, bank statements, credit card statements and bill invoices.

The relationships cited are not meant to be interpreted as including real friendships. The Bible teaches us that *"there is a friend that sticketh closer than a brother"* (Proverbs 18:24). Therefore, our real friends, as well as devoted family members, will always be with us, and are meant to go with us into eternity. However, nothing is more suffocating and stifling to our soul and spirit than our physical hold on that which our soul and spirit has declared dead to our divine purpose and mission in the earth.

Our mastery of the skill of letting go is closely aligned to our disciplined obedience to the spiritual law known as the vacuum law. I was first introduced to this law in the writings of Catherine Ponder, the well-known author and teacher of spiritual and metaphysical principles. The vacuum law states that life abhors a vacuum. Therefore, if we want to grow and expand, create and receive anew, then we must create a vacuum in that place where we want to grow and expand and create and receive anew.

I still smile when I recall a television broadcast I watched some years ago featuring the well-known teacher and pastor, fondly known as "Reverend Ike" by his parishioners. At some point during the

52

televised service, Reverend Ike interviewed a very attractive woman who acknowledged that she was desirous of finding a husband, but wasn't having much success in doing so. With microphone in hand, Rev. Ike responded, without missing a beat, "What is the status of your closet?" The woman looked at him somewhat askance. Rev. Ike continued, "Is there room in your closet for a new husband's clothes?" Both the woman and audience began to laugh. When the woman recovered from her surprise at such a question, she readily admitted that at the present time her closets were all full with her own clothes. "Well then," said Rev. Ike, "go home and make room in your closet so your husband will have somewhere to put his clothes."

A later televised program featured the woman who wished for a husband and her new husband. I shall always remember this testimony as a dramatic illustration of the demonstration of the effective combination of the vacuum law and the ultimate skill of letting go.

"Call Those Things That Be Not As Though They Were"

In his classic work, *The Science of Successful Living*, (Cornerstone Library: New York, 1957, pp. 15-17) Charles Raymond Barker, D.D., the late, dynamic and eloquent Minister of the First Church of Religious Science in New York City, relates the story of a woman who came to him for counseling during what is known as the Great Depression of the 1930's in our country.

I first read the story during my law school years. My family and I were also privileged to attend Sunday church services in Alice Tully Hall in Lincoln Center where Dr. Barker was the featured speaker each Sunday. The story made an unforgettable and lasting impression on me. Dr. Barker describes the woman that came to see him in 1932 as almost destitute. Her specific request was that he "show her a way of changing her consciousness so she could again have prosperity and freedom in money."

Dr. Barker said he asked only one question: "What is the one thing above all others that you would like to do?" The woman replied that she had always wanted to be a pastry specialist. However, in 1932, jobs as a regular baker, let alone a pastry specialist, were not to be found. Nevertheless, Dr. Barker said, "Then go ahead and do it...If we together subconsciously accept the idea that you can be this, then every door will open for you to do it." He then gave her an affirmation to recite and meditate on emphasizing that nothing is too hard for God; that He "knows neither depression nor impossibility" and that she was "free from all fear and established in all faith."

Dr. Barker writes that, while he and this courageous woman believed her desire to be sound, they recognized that by the world's standards, and in the face of existing economic circumstances, "her desire was nothing less than impractical, if not impossible." Nevertheless, in ways that far exceeded human comprehension of what was possible, a noted manufacturer of flours arranged a one week pastry school at the Waldorf-Astoria Hotel in New York City. Amazingly, she was one of those chosen out of thousands of applicants.

But the story does not end there. After being notified of her selection, she hitch-hiked four hundred miles to New York City. After successfully completing the course, Dr. Barker concludes that "she was considered so unusual that she was offered a job as a pastry specialist in one of the few wealthy clubs able to survive during the depression. She has been constantly employed in that type of work at the finest clubs and hotels ever since, receiving a large salary."

Here we have the example of a woman out of work in the midst of the Great Depression, and, as a result, experiencing tremendous need in every area of her life. Things looked bleak all around and she saw no way out of her life threatening dilemma.

However, what she needed most, she already possessed. And that is, she knew enough about God's truth and spiritual principles, that she decided that if some how she could make her way to Dr. Barker's office and have him agree with her as to the deepest desires of her heart, her circumstances would begin to turn around and she would be back on the path to prosperity and freedom in money.

This brave woman, with the help and guidance of Dr. Barker, exercised the spiritual power that is possessed by all believers through the indwelling of the Holy Spirit that "...*calleth those things which be not as though they were*" (Romans 4:17). You, too, can do what this woman of faith did. You can cast off the luxury of fear, doubt or failure. You can project the desires of your heart with authority. You can allow no one to discourage you. You can keep your mind and emotions stayed on God.

Every day we have the same choice as did this courageous woman. We can call into existence the desires of our heart. Or, we can succumb to unwanted circumstances, through our failure to speak into our lives all that comes with His vision for our lives, under girded by His provision.

"Our Small and Puny Prayer Requests Insult and Dishonor God"

Nothing insults and dishonors our Heavenly Father as much as our small and puny prayer requests. We have been created by a God that is unlimited in His power, knowledge and presence in our lives. We are the precious children of the Most High God.

Our concept of impossible has no meaning to Him. Our acceptance of incurable diseases and poverty has no meaning to Him. Our tolerance of fear and intimidation has no meaning to Him. Our ability to see others as giants and ourselves as grasshoppers has no meaning to Him. The rivers that we are unable to cross, and mountains too steep for us to climb have no meaning to Him.

Someone has said that we come to the Father with our small cup to be filled when He owns the whole ocean. Not all of us come with cup in hand. There are those of us whose faith is a little greater. We come with a bucket instead of a cup. And then there are those who are courageous enough to come to the ocean with a wheel barrel, apparently recognizing that "God can only do for us what He can do through us." No matter the size of our containers, God wants to give us so much more than our puny requests dictate.

Sometimes our prayers are not answered simply because our requests are not big enough. They are too small and puny. They insult and dishonor God. For example, we are praying for next month's rent when, in addition to next month's rent, God wants us to ask Him for ownership of our own home. Or we are praying that the new medicine works, while God wants us to ask Him for the healing of our body. We might be praying and struggling to meet the monthly mortgage payment, while God wants us to ask Him for the payoff of the mortgage altogether.

You might be in the midst of praying for God to bring the right companion into your life. But God wants you to pray the larger prayer that seeks divine companionship with the Father, Son and Holy Spirit. A right relationship with the Father attracts and makes all other relationships right— that is, if you're willing to be patient, and give God time to unfold His plan for this part of your life.

To be able to accurately evaluate whether answers to your prayer requests are being hamstrung by the size and significance of your requests, I highly recommend that you begin to keep two file folders back-to-back. The first should be a folder entitled *Prayer Requests*. The second should be a folder entitled *Answers to Prayer*. These records will enable you to better see if you are giving due reverence, through your prayer requests, to the Most High God, or if your requests, while however sincere, insult and dishonor *the God Who has promised to give you what you ask for and— if He doesn't have it— to make it for you* (John 14:13-14).

Worration

My grandmother, Rosa Lee Bradley Washington Terry, knew — and then did — what most people apparently don't know and consequently don't do. Mama knew that underneath it all, God had created her to be an artist. She knew, moreover, that as an artist, God had anointed her with the artist's power to create. She knew that she had the power to create delicious meals from scratch; a home atmosphere that was filled with loving and encouraging words; and a home environment that was always open, warm and welcoming to her family, friends and church members.

But more importantly, Mama intuitively recognized that she had the power to create her own personal dictionary and vocabulary. She had the power to create her own definitions of words commonly used in everyday conversation. I don't ever recall Mama using the word "worry." For Mama, her word to describe that state of being anxious and afraid, for reasons perceived and unperceived, was always *worration*.

It never dawned on me to ask Mama why she insisted on using worration when everybody else used "worry." It could be that Mama thought that the use of worry was just plain unsuitable to describe that heavy condition of mental distress and anxiety over some impending or anticipated occurrence. Perhaps it was because Mama always used her own vocabulary made up of her own words. Everybody that Mama dealt with seemed to understand this about Mama; and as far as I know, no one in Mama's circle of family, friends, co-workers or acquaintances ever challenged her or called her on it. In fact, Mama's creation and use of her own vocabulary seemed to generate a certain quiet and understood respect from others.

I believe that Mama considered the articulated sound of worry as a spoken word as just being too inappropriate for that actual state of mind when one is worried to death. Worry sounded too light, lilting and flighty. She often said that worration killed more people than any other disease. On the heels of describing the fatal impact of worration on the mind and body, Mama would quickly add that

that is why you have to wear your problems, as much as possible, as loose garments.

Mama would certainly agree with the teaching of the Rev. Dr. Tony Evans, Senior Pastor of Oak Cliff Bible Fellowship and President of The Urban Alternative. In one of his radio broadcasts, Dr. Evans metaphorically defined worry as follows: "Worry is a rocking chair. It keeps you moving, it just doesn't take you anywhere." I consider this to be an accurate definition of worry. Too many of us, through faithless living, put the "w" in worry and then wonder why our lives seem to stay in a holding position and our dreams remain dried up and deferred.

All worry is fueled by fear. We worry that we will not have the money to meet certain obligations; that we might lose our jobs; that we won't be able to pay the rent on time; or that we might be diagnosed with a terminal illness.

If we own our business, we worry that we'll run out of clients and then out of capital. If we have been blessed with children, we worry that they will not discover God's perfect will and purpose for their lives. Our worry is often rooted in Murphy's Law which states, in part, that "Anything that could go wrong will go wrong."

The Scriptures tell us that, *"If God clothes the lilies of the field that are here today and gone tomorrow; and feeds the birds of the air that neither toil nor labor, how much more will he clothe and take care of us—His beloved sons and daughters?"* (Matthew 6:26-33 NIV).

Once upon a time, I could have easily qualified for first place or runner-up in a champion worrier contest. During those times when everything in my life that could go wrong, did go wrong, I learned to trust God with all that I held dear. In so doing, I learned that I could not trust God and worry at the same time.

Consequently, the more I trusted God, the less I worried; and the less I worried, the more opportunity I had to trust God. Moreover, when the proverbial rug had been pulled out from under me in almost every area of my life, God used these dark times, that I later saw as sacred and precious, to teach me that He is more than sufficient to answer my every prayer and meet my every need.

In the midst of difficult circumstances, God began to teach me the most sacred of all His secrets. He began to teach me that he is faithful. I did not have to let go of my circumstances. My circumstances had to let go of me. I knew, without a doubt, that only God could intervene and turn everything around. He did in ways that proved my faith, purified my life and prepared me for the dawn of a new day in which He would use me for maximum service in the Kingdom of God.

It is interesting that most of us who have been blessed with godly parents seldom, if ever, question whether our parents, if able, will come through for us; or whether they will deliver on promises made. We have a need. We go to our father or mother for help. Or our mother or father offers help without our having to ask. We don't have to plead with our mother or father for help. They see the need. They meet the need. After all, we are their children and they love us. Of course they will help us in any way that they can.

Similarly, our heavenly Father is waiting for us to come to Him for help with whatever it is that we need. God, in His word, has told us that, "*If we, being evil, know how to give good gifts to our children, how much more our heavenly Father wants to give good gifts to those who love Him*" (Matthew 7:11).

Worration, more than anything else, is an insult to our heavenly Father. Our worration says to the Father, "I'm not sure that you can." This attitude dismisses the omnipotence of God. Our worration also says, "Even if you can, I'm not sure that you will." This attitude discounts the unconditional love of the Father. He is thus regarded as no more than a capricious conductor of the cosmos. Our worration further says, "God obviously doesn't know what's going on here or He'd stop it." This attitude ignores the omniscience of the Father.

Worration says in response to our circumstances of hardship, pain and trial, "I am all alone with no one to help me." This attitude fails to factor in the omnipresence of the Almighty. And finally, our worration unfortunately focuses on the power of people and not on the sovereignty of the Savior and His sole ability to do exceedingly, abundantly more than we could ever ask or imagine.

Divine power shall always preempt human power and prove, again and again, to a wicked and watching world, that our God is not a capricious conductor of the cosmos, but the Great I AM that forever beckons us to leave our comfortable rocking chairs and says to His beloved "...*concerning the work of my hands command ye me*" (Isaiah 45:11). Our loving Father will then take us to places we've never dreamed nor imagined. And finally, the Lord promises us that "*Thou shalt also decree a thing, and it shall be established unto thee, and the light shall shine upon thy ways*" (Job 22:28).

"Not Forgiving Is Like Taking Poison And Expecting It To Kill The Other Person"

Would you take poison and expect it to kill someone else? Absolutely not! In fact, you would consider such an idea preposterous. But that is exactly what we do when we refuse to forgive another person for some perceived or actual wrong they've done to us.

When it comes to forgiving another who has, in some way wounded us, we are all too human. Our first reaction is to get even. We are determined to make the other person pay for hurting us. This results in a spirit of unforgiveness that fosters a root of bitterness.

Nothing poisons our spirit, soul and body as does the unforgiveness that we hang onto and nurse. It wreaks more havoc in our lives than does any other negative emotion. It spews out into the environment and circumstances of our lives and contaminates everything that it contacts and touches.

It has been wisely stated by an astute observer that "*Unforgiveness is like taking poison and expecting it to kill the other person.*" There are no words that substitute for such precious, if not sacred, counsel. The other person that is due the receipt of our unforgiveness is usually not affected at all by our spirit and attitude of unforgiveness. Typically, in fact, the individual is not even aware that we are harboring the negative emotion of unforgiveness.

In the area of prayer, countless numbers of pastors and prayer warriors point to unforgiveness as the single block, more than any other, to answered prayer in the life of the Christian.

Forgiveness of others is the purifying catalyst that swings wide the gates of heaven when we approach the throne of grace and mercy for answers to our multitude of prayer petitions. Doors of every imaginable opportunity in life come dependent on God-given hinges. However, often these same doors remain firmly sealed and closed when, as believers, our unforgiveness and a bitter spirit effectively corrodes the hinges. Whereas, forgiveness and a sweet spirit keeps the hinges oiled and smooth, allowing them to swing wide open, provided the open doors serve to keep God's will, plan and purpose paramount.

In Matthew 6:12-15, the word of God teaches us that we must forgive those who trespass against us, use, and even abuse us. If we refuse to forgive, we are like a sick person hooked up to an intravenous feeding tube filled with poison. We are forgiven our trespasses, *"as we forgive others"* that trespass against us. In other words, we can't have one before and without the other. Moreover, if we do not forgive others for the wrong they commit against us, our Father will not forgive us for the wrongs we have committed.

The medical profession refers to certain diseases as silent killers. Included in these are usually high blood pressure and hypertension. The damage that is being done by these illnesses is invisible to the naked eye. Obvious pain to the individual is also absent, and so the damage is referred to as silent. However, the damage to the blood vessels and to the heart, unchecked by medical treatment, severely threatens the very life of the person.

Unforgiveness is also a silent killer. It is a spiritual condition that, overtime, results in emotional and even physical illness. While unforgiveness is not considered a medical condition, it must be treated just the same. The antidote for unforgiveness is a simple prayer to the Holy Spirit, asking Him to forgive, through you, that person that you are unable to forgive. Our prayer for the Holy Spirit to forgive through us must be prayed regularly and relentlessly.

If you have struggled with unforgiveness, or if you even have trouble with the metaphor of unforgiveness as a deadly poison to your body, the prayer of forgiveness is critical and mandatory to the health of your body and to the eternal salvation of your soul.

The Holy Spirit can do, through us, what we cannot do for ourselves. But we must give Him a chance. We give Him a chance when we ask Him to forgive through us. If our prayer is sincere and persistent, we shall one day be amazed at how the power of the Holy Spirit has softened our hearts; transformed our minds; and cleansed our spirits of the poison that is unforgiveness.

We shall discover that we are now spiritually free, as we have never been before. Now we are emotionally available for God to use us in a mighty way to carry out His magnificent plan for our life and for the lives of others that we touch through our holy walk through the world.

"You Are Powerful Beyond Measure"

Has anyone ever told you that *"You are powerful beyond measure?"* That's right. You are so powerful that the depth and breadth of your power cannot be measured in human terms. Your power is the power of the Holy Spirit that is within you.

Most of us are so dominated by fear, that we are blinded to the power that is resident within us. But Paul tells us in 2 Timothy 1:7: *"For God hath not given us the spirit of fear; but of power, and of love, and of a sound mind."*

Author Marianne Williamson, in *A Return to Love* (HarperCollins Publishers: New York, NY, 1992, p.165), speaks brilliantly of our power and the fear that often restrains our power when she states:

> "Our deepest fear is not that we are inadequate.
> Our deepest fear is that *we are powerful beyond measure.*
> It is our light, not our darkness, that most frightens us.
> We ask ourselves, who am I to be brilliant,
> gorgeous, talented, and fabulous?
> Actually, who are you not to be?
> You are a child of God.
> Your playing small does not serve the world.
> There is nothing enlightened about shrinking
> so that other people won't feel insecure around you.
> We are all meant to shine, as children do. We were born to
> make manifest the glory of God that is within us.
> It is not just in some of us, it is in everyone.
> And as we let our own light shine, we unconsciously
> give other people permission to do the same.
> As we are liberated from our own fear,
> our presence automatically liberates others."

Imagine what our lives would resemble if we knew that we were powerful; and even more so, if we knew that *we were powerful beyond measure.* Imagine the goals we would set for ourselves, the millions of lives we would influence; the *"even greater work"* that we would do, if we really believed that we have received power from God. How long can you feel inadequate and stay depressed with the knowledge of the power of God bubbling and percolating in you—the temple of the Holy Spirit?

Imagine the expanse of our success if we were convinced that we have been imbued with power from on high; power that guarantees the extraordinary execution of our divine mission and assignment.

Think of our attitude regarding failure. Depending on the extent of our failure and whether it is subject to public viewing, it typically conjures up feelings of disappointment, discouragement, fear, frustration, and at the extreme end, depression and despair.

On the other hand, spiritual growth and maturity are designed to enable us to see failure for what it really is; that is, to see the truth about failure. It is no more than the child in you falling, and getting up again, as you learn to walk on a new path of experience that is bringing you closer to the achievement of some particular goal, or the mastery of some particular skill.

More importantly, failure is often God's call to us, challenging us to learn to listen with our eyes, as well as our inner ear, and hear what the Holy Spirit is whispering to our heart and soul. Sometimes you'll be surprised to hear: "*My child, 'You are powerful beyond measure.' Therefore, be obedient and stop making excuses; stop making excuses; stop making excuses.*"

And to that I say: *Go now and do the greater work that only you can do; that only you have been empowered from on high to do.*

See God In Everything

If there is one divine principle and promise that will meet your every need, calm your every fear, and sustain you during the most difficult times in your life, while you await the realization of some cherished dream or deeply desired answer to prayer, it is the biblical principle based on 1 Samuel 3:18 (NIV) which states: *"He is the Lord; let him do what is good in his eyes."*

This biblical principle is beautifully espoused by L.B. Cowman when she writes: *"If I see God in everything, He will calm and color everything I see!"* Moreover, she continues, "Seeing God in everything is the only thing that will make me loving and patient with people who annoy and trouble me. Then I will see others as the instruments God uses to accomplish His tender and wise purpose for me, and I will even find myself inwardly thanking them for the blessing they have become to me. Nothing but seeing God will completely put an end to all complaining and thoughts of rebellion" (Op. Cit., p. 353).

No matter what the circumstances that we face, we shall not despair if we follow the wise counsel of Dr. Betty Peoples, the powerful Bible teacher and the Presiding Prelate of Jericho City of Praise, in Landover, Maryland, when she teaches: *"If what you see is not what you saw, then what you see is temporary."*

We must begin by remembering that this entire universe and everything in it was made by God. He is, at all times and in all ways, in absolute control. Nothing, that is, no thing occurs without His direction or permission. Therefore, you must see God even in every wrong that is done to you. In lay parlance, for most of us, "this is where the rubber meets the road."

When disaster hits, or tough times won't turn us loose; colleagues conspire against us and we lose our job; a dear friend is killed in an automobile accident; we lose custody of our child; a beloved spouse betrays our trust; the doctor's diagnosis leaves little room for cure; our finances are in shambles; we're given a pink slip right before Thanksgiving; our friends desert us during times of crises; we're falsely accused and our good name is slandered—it is at these times that we all have the tendency to engage in plaintive prayers of, "God why did you let this happen?" or "God, when are you going to get me out of this mess?" God simply waits until our perspective of our hellish circumstances rises to that of our elder brother Job in his prayerful praise of the Most High God: *"The Lord gave and the Lord has taken away; may the name of the Lord be praised"* (Job:1:21).

Rest assured that God always hears our prayers. But His "... *thoughts are not your thoughts, neither are your ways my ways, saith the Lord"* (Isaiah 55:8). He is a perfect God. And even though we are made in His image and likeness, we are, nevertheless, imperfect children.

The wise and godly man and woman, when beset with the garden variety of trouble in their lives, no matter how exasperating or painful, yields in faith to the mighty hands of the Master Potter and remains still on the Potter's wheel until he or she has been molded and made after God's will. The Christian who is Christlike in his character, conduct and conversation remains steadfast during seasons of hardship, tests and trials. He has a firm grip on the promise of Romans 8:28: *"And we know that all things work together for good to them that love God, to them who are the called according to his purpose."*

The center and circumference of the Christian's faith rests on the loving promise of God, articulated by David and found in Psalm 34:7: *"the angel of the Lord encampeth round about them that fear him, and delivereth them."*

The author, Hannah Whitall Smith, in her classic work, *A Christian's Secret to A Happy Life* (Whitaker House: New Kensington, PA, 1983, 2005, p. 81) offers her rationale, so beautifully espoused, for the Christian's resolve to see God in everything: *"If the Lord is your helper, how can you fear what man may do unto you? There is no man in this world, nor company of men, who can touch you, unless your God, in whom you trust, lets them..."*

The Price Is Nails

There can be no coronation without crucifixion. There can be no crucifixion without a cross. There can be no cross without nails.

Sooner or later, no matter how much money you may have, what your social status in the community might be; no matter how many degrees you may have; no matter your connections with the in crowd or the politically connected; no matter what kind of car you drive; or whether you live in a mansion or a loft; if it hasn't happened already; life is going to get you where it hurts. The bottom is going to fall out. The walls are going to cave in. The top is going to come tumbling down.

We avoid our desperately needed participation in certain situations in life, offering as our explanation the fact that we don't have the big picture. In actuality, we're stating the situation in reverse. It's because we know, all too well, the ultimate price of a particular pursuit that causes us to back off. We know the price is nails.

Our attitude, quite understandable, is, "Who needs the pain, the pressure and the problems brought on by nails?" Nevertheless, our personalized, designer-made crucibles await each of us. The only questions are "What?" "When?" "Where?" "Whom?" Even if we spend the bulk of our lives engaged in avoidance responses, sooner or later, at the end of the day, nails await us.

Nails come in many forms and circumstances. Almost daily, my clients remind me of this spiritual truth. Dr. Acosta's pending divorce was prompted by the nails hammered into her body and soul by her abusive husband. For almost twenty years, she was subjected to a level of domestic violence that knew no boundaries.

Tina's nails stem from the abandonment by her baby's father, who happens to be, chronologically, a child himself. My church member's sister just received the kidney she had been waiting for for seven years. The involuntary donor was a college student who drank himself to death at a fraternity house on the campus of a local college. The sister's nails were the seven years of endless waiting for the phone to ring with the hospital calling to ask whether she still wanted a transplant.

Christian author L.B. Cowman poetically teaches us that "We are born into the world with our own unique cross to bear. If we manage to escape our cross today, rest assured, another one will be waiting to take its place tomorrow. But if we restrain our escapist inclinations, and this, admittedly, takes a lot of grit and guts, and begin to see our personal crucibles as Christ centered, we are guaranteed the victory of a resurrected life in Christ Jesus."

"This Trip Is Necessary"

There are times in our life when we must take trips that we would prefer to either reschedule or cancel altogether. These trips often expand into seasons when we must endure hardship, pressure and pain. These are times designed by the Father to prepare us for the remainder of our life's journey, including the blessings archived for us on earth, and the rewards that shall be ours in Heaven. Moreover, these are trips that conform us to the image and likeness of His Dear Son.

Are you on a trip of separation and divorce from your spouse? Or perhaps your current trip is one of grief over the loss of a loved one. It may be that you have had to endure a trip that involved some public disgrace, humiliation and social ostracism. Your trip might consist of a time of hospitalization or incarceration. It may be a trip of having to parent a delinquent child. Or you may be on a trip with a loved one who is in bondage to repeated addiction. Your trip could be the loss of employment through no fault of your own; or having to oversee the loss of a business you gave your all to. Or sometimes the most grievous trip of all is that of betrayal by a trusted friend.

You would have given anything to avoid some of the trips you've had to take in the past, or the trip God has you on at the present time. You've probably said, at various times, "If only God would let this cup pass this one time, I won't ask Him for anything else." But God knows what is best for us and He determines the direction, destination and duration of our trips. He has told us in no uncertain terms in His word, *"For I know the thoughts that I think toward you, saith the Lord, thoughts of peace, and not of evil, to give you an expected end"* (Jeremiah 29:11).

It is the trenches and fox holes, the dunghills and strongholds; the battering storms and raging winds that God uses to mold and make us into men and women of unwavering faith, stalwart resolve, and courageous commitment needed to trust and obey the Master in every detail of His call on our life.

Many years ago, through her incomparable, albeit brief, work entitled *"Mental Equivalents,"* I was introduced to Louise L. Hay, well-known teacher and lecturer in Metaphysics and bestselling author. In *The Power Is Within You* (Hay House, Inc.: Carlsbad, CA, 1991, p. 92) Hay shares with her readers the following poignant message from "*Emmanuel's Book*," (Bantam Books: New York, 1987, p.116):

"The question to Emmanuel is:
'How do we experience painful circumstances
without becoming embittered by them?'"

"And Emmanuel's reply is:
'By seeing them as lessons and not as retribution.
Trust life, my friends. However far afield life seems
to take you, *this trip is necessary.* You have come to
traverse a wide terrain of experience in order to verify
where truth lies and where your distortion is in
that terrain. You will then be able to return to your
home center, your soul self, refreshed and wiser.'"

Trips that we would never have planned are, at first, and under-standably, unwelcome, then denied, and often fiercely resisted. Have you ever put your foot down and boldly told God in your own words and way what amounted to, "No, I'm not going on this trip!" Or as our contemporaries express it: "I'm not going to go there!" It is at these times that God challenges us to pattern our behavior after His beloved Son.

When faced with the prospect of the cross, Jesus specifically asked the Father "*Saying, Father, if thou be willing, remove this cup from me: nevertheless not my will, but thine, be done*" (Luke 22:42). However, Jesus surrendered to the will of His Father, even to the prospect of the bitter cup of His own crucifixion and death. Jesus provides for us the classic model of trust and obedience to the Father's plan and purpose for the child of God.

Where would we be if Jesus had resisted the specific call on His life by the Father? Where would we be if Jesus had refused to shed His precious blood for the redemption of our sins?

We, too, must adjust to those trips in our life where the contents of the cup are nothing less than bitter. While we are enduring the bitter taste, remember that our Heavenly Father schedules the trip. It is He that fills our cup, even to overflowing. He loves us unconditionally and is infinitely wise. He always, always has our best interest at heart. And most of all, our Heavenly Father is in absolute, sovereign control of the entire universe.

When we obediently embark on trips deemed necessary by the Father, our souls will be so deeply nourished by the Holy Spirit that we shall be able to *"Consider it a sheer gift, friends, when tests and challenges come at you from all sides. You know that under pressure, your faith-life is forced into the open and shows its true colors. So don't try to get out of anything prematurely. Let it do its work so you become mature and well-developed, not deficient in any way* "(James 1:2-4 MSG).

"Be Kind To Others.
Everyone You Meet Is Fighting A Hard Battle"

Without fail, each year, I know that I shall receive, from a close, childhood family friend, a warm birthday greeting, either in the mail or by telephone. A few years ago, this dear friend penned the following words inside my birthday card: *"Be kind to others. Everyone you meet is fighting a hard battle."*

What if you knew, as does my friend, that behind the smiling faces and material fronts, everyone you meet is fighting a hard battle? For some, the battle has been created by their hands. For others, the battle has been instigated by Satan. For others, the battle has been ordained by God, and is therefore, our divine destiny. Yes, there are some battles we are destined to fight. These are battles that, try as we will, we shall not escape.

The important factor to realize is that no matter how calm, confident and serene our meeting one with another, a battle rages all around us. It is the battle to annihilate our spirit and our faith and capture our eternal souls.

As followers of Christ, our position in battle must always be on our knees on the inside, at the throne of grace, petitioning Jesus Christ who sits at the right hand of the Father, interceding on our behalf, in the warfare that comes with the territory of being a child of God. Kneeling on the inside, in the faith-fight mode, must always be our posture, even in the heat of the battle.

As children of God, we don't cross each other's path by chance. The times and circumstances of our meetings with one another have been orchestrated by God before the foundations of the world were laid. When we come into each other's presence, we must use our spiritual sight to see that we are all going through deep waters and fiery furnaces—at some level. We might not talk about it, cry about it or shout about it in public. Instead, we follow Christ's command that we come into our house, shut the door and pray to the Father in secret. The Father, in secret, hears our prayers, and then, on His clock, rewards us openly.

Our mere presence in each other's company would result in healing, wholeness and sometimes perfect answers to our prayers, if we would begin to see ourselves as spiritual warriors on spiritual battle fields; armed with *"weapons of our warfare (that) are not carnal, but mighty through God to the pulling down of strong holds..."* (2 Corinthians 10:4); always fighting spiritual battles that are not ours, but God's; always fighting the good fight of faith; knowing that victory has already been declared by God as ours, and therefore, knowing that, in the end, we win.

Everyone you meet is fighting a hard battle. We are all battle-fatigued, and sometimes even gun shy—we've been shot at so many times. Therefore, Paul admonishes us, *"And be ye kind to one another, tenderhearted, forgiving one another, even as God for Christ's sake hath forgiven you"* (Ephesians 4:32).

"Love Is Eternal"

This essay is intended as a tribute to Hardy, my beloved late husband, marital partner, best friend, soul mate and confidant. This essay's title is taken from Irving Stone's popular bestseller, *Love Is Eternal*, given to me many years ago by my father upon the book's initial publication. While I cannot recall the details of the story of Abraham Lincoln and his wife, Mary Todd Lincoln, as recounted by Stone, I consider the book's title fitting in every way to describe my seventeen year marriage to Hardy.

As husband and wife, we were at all times dynamically engaged in an authentic, vital and refreshing marital relationship. At no time did we just cohabit as a married couple. We faced the world as one in the good times and during the difficult times. We loved each other. We were committed to each other and to our respective dreams and aspirations. We helped each other. We rejoiced in each other's accomplishments. We were ever mindful that if the Holy Spirit were to dwell in our home, we would have to create and maintain a home environment dominated by peace and love for one another and for all those that would enter therein. Our life was not free of storms. We had our share of heartbreak, disappointment, suffering and trial. Nevertheless, in all of our times of severe testing and trials, we saw nothing but the hand of God. And faithful to His Word, God never left our side as we faced the windstorms head on, always steadfast in our faith.

What made all the difference in our marriage was that Hardy was such a good man, a refined man, a man for all seasons, and a godly man. When I think of Hardy, I am reminded of 1 John 4:8 which states, *"Whoever does not love does not know God, because God is love."* Hardy was a man of deep love and commitment. Hardy also knew God. Hardy was pure gold and together we made our home a heaven. Some years ago, when Hardy was featured in the "Doers Profile" column of *The Washington Times* newspaper, his "last words" quoted were: "I have tried to love and help my fellow man." I can attest, unequivocally, that he accomplished his goal.

My loss of Hardy was so devastating that even though I consider myself as never at a loss for words, I could find no words to describe the depth of my sorrow and grief. I still can't. Hardy's Homegoing Service was held on a beautiful Saturday morning in August, 2004. By the next Tuesday morning, I was too ill with a cold and congestion to get out of the bed. As the day progressed, my feeble condition worsened with unrelenting headaches and the loss of my physical strength. I had finally collapsed under the grief of my loss of Hardy. At some point Tuesday evening, I fell asleep from sheer exhaustion.

About three o'clock the next morning, I awoke abruptly from a vivid dream. In the opening scene of the dream, I saw myself lying in a hospital bed. In the bed next to mine was my next door neighbor. All of a sudden, Hardy burst through the door to our hospital room! He was handsomely clothed in his signature dress of a sharp, dark, navy blue, pin-striped suit, and a beautiful tie and shirt. I could feel the tremendous power and strength that exuded from his presence. I immediately rose up from my bed pillow and cried out, "Hardy! Hardy, you're alive! I can't wait to tell everybody that you're alive!" Then just as suddenly as he had appeared, he was gone. I then woke up. I was so happy.

The Lord had allowed Hardy to come and see about me. Hardy knew that I was sick. He had felt my suffering and grief over his passing. Visiting me in my dream was his way of letting me know that he is very much alive and that I don't have to worry about him. He's fine. He's well. He's no longer sick. Praise God. Hardy's appearance and concern was saying that I don't have to grieve over him; that I don't have to allow my grief to put me in bed and keep me down; that I must get up and carry on with the assignment God has given me: the speaking, writing, teaching assignment. From that moment on, I felt energized and empowered to obey whatever orders I considered to be straight from the Father's playbook for my life. I was on my feet again by Friday.

Since having this powerful dream, I have been able to put my grief on the shelf. God allowed Hardy to visit me to assure me that, indeed, he is at home in glory, and I have no need to grieve his loss any longer. Instead, I must rejoice that Hardy, although *"absent from the body, is now present with the Lord"* (2 Corinthians 5:8). I still have talks with Hardy, usually just to tell him how much I miss him, his unwavering support of all of my many endeavors and the many wonderful times we shared.

God used the dream to remind me that He knows my need and that He meets my need in ways that no man or woman can.

Thank you, Jesus.

"When You Pray, Move Your Feet"

There is an old Quaker saying that states: "When you pray, move your feet." When was the last time you prayed and did nothing? For example, when we're praying for a specific need, God will answer through His Holy Spirit. The Holy Spirit will speak to us, direct us, guide us, caution us, warn us, persuade us, encourage and strengthen us.

He will tell us when to speak and when to keep silent; when to move and when to stay put; when to hold and when to fold; when to go out and when to come in; when to open your arms wide and when to keep them folded; when to respond to a request and when to just listen.

If it is a job that we need, the Holy Spirit might tell us to: "Contact this office. Call this person. Read the newspaper employment section everyday. Tell those in your circle of friends and acquaintances that you're looking for work. Attend this job fair. Let this person help you with your resume. Work part-time until you can work full-time. Take what you can get until you can get what you want."

As Dr. Charles Stanley is fond of saying, "God is sitting on ready, waiting to answer the prayers of His children." The reason God wants us to move our feet when we pray is because God has all of His people out in the vineyards ready to do His bidding in having our prayers answered. But these people are not coming to the front door of our apartment or our home. We have to get on the highways and byways. We have to get out into the market place if we are going to get our prayers answered.

The Enemy wants you to sit at home and do nothing. He is pleased when you are in such dire straits that you can't even get out of bed. He is overjoyed that you consider the power of your God to be limited and insignificant in the face of the demands being made upon you.

However, the children of God who pray and move their feet when the storms are raging all about are blessed beyond measure. God, without fail, vindicates their unshakable faith in His power before a waiting and watching world, *provided* they will stand and know that God is able.

The Problem Is Simply That We Won't

In his classic and timeless devotional entitled *My Utmost For His Highest,* Oswald Chambers states: "The problem that most of us are cursed with is simply that *we won't.*" We won't obey God and leave all the consequences to Him. We won't dare to follow the leading of the Holy Spirit as He speaks to our hearts. We won't defy the odds and follow Jesus wherever the path may lead.

To refuse to obey God is to be cursed. It is to open the door to great evil entering our lives. To be cursed is to be blocked from receiving all the blessings that God has stored up just for us. The consequences of our disobedience are disappointment, failure, hardship, loss and pain. The problem of disobedience to God's laws and divine commands to us can't be solved by another. Each individual must answer God's call and promptly obey Him.

Obedience to God is so significant that it has a domino effect on our lives. *We take care of God's business, and God takes care of our business.* Without our help or interference, we sometimes witness, in awe, hard problems being resolved by nothing less than a Higher Hand.

Our disobedience is typically rooted in arrogance. God tells us to do something. We know in our hearts that we have heard from God. But our arrogance pipes up and rehearses all the reasons why what God has told us to do either can't be done or can't be done by us. We cower to our own arrogance and disobey God.

Our disobedience to God's command is also rooted in fear. We are afraid that even with God's help, however omnipotent, omniscient and omnipresent; we just might not be able to pull it off. We play God cheap every day and never give it another thought. After all, He is just the Creator of the Universe, the alpha and omega of all existence. But the world has conditioned us to require so much more than that.

We forget the two characteristics about God that should never be forgotten. The first is that He is able. Able to do what? He is able to do exceedingly, abundantly above all that we could ever ask or imagine. The second is that He is faithful. Faithful to what? He is

81

faithful to His Word and to the promises of His Word. Whatever He said is so. Whatever He promised has already been delivered. He is a man that does not, cannot lie.

God wants to pour into our lives the blessings He has stored up for you and for me. But He cannot do it unless we allow Him. And we allow Him by being obedient to His precious Word to us. God's response to obedience is abundant blessings. But sometimes the journey to abundant blessings can get rough and rocky. So fasten the seat belts of God's Word all around you.

The path of obedience has been skillfully and lovingly made by the Father just for you. Therefore, to paraphrase *Jonathan Livingston Seagull*, you must begin the trip to your divine destiny by "knowing that you have already arrived."

"We Don't Know What To Do,
But Our Eyes Are Upon You"

When faced with an insurmountable problem, and surrounded on all sides by seemingly impossible circumstances, and facts that scream "there's nothing you can do," remember that there's only one thing that you need to do—and that is to fall on your knees and pray the prayer of surrender: "Have your way, Lord." In other words, surrender the outcome of the problem to the Master to do with as He pleases. Commit to bow to His will, His way and His time in the matter.

Even when you think you know the right resolution, give your dilemma over to the Father. He knows better. He sees farther. He understands deeper. His plan and His purpose are perfect. He makes no mistakes. He loves us unconditionally. And we are made for His glory and honor, and in the image of His Dear Son, Jesus Christ.

When Jesus told Peter to come to Him, Peter began to walk on the water, his eyes focused on the Master. But then he became distracted, taking his eyes off Jesus when the winds began to blow and the waves began to billow (Matthew 14: 29-30).

In an instant, Peter gave more attention to the winds and waves than to Jesus. Fear took over and Peter bowed to his fear rather than bowing to the power and presence of the Almighty God, the Creator of the winds and waves.

In the Second Book of Chronicles of the Old Testament, King Jehoshaphat is faced with three different armies coming against him and his people. Jehoshaphat quickly acknowledged the Lord of all and in his historic prayer said to God: *"O our God, wilt thou not judge them? For we have no might against this great company that cometh against us; neither know we what to do: but our eyes are upon thee"* (2 Chronicles 20:12). In other words, Jehoshaphat was saying "You are more than equal to whatever the task at hand to save us from this vicious attack by not just one, but three armies all coming against us at the same time." Jehoshaphat and his people surrendered to God's will, God's way and God's time. And God rewarded their faith with victory over their enemies.

83

You, dear child of God, may be in a situation that is figuratively similar to that of Jehoshaphat. Not only is there one army, but three armies coming against you at the same time. It has been said that troubles never come one at a time, but in multiples of three or more. I believe that God ordains or allows multifaceted problems to teach us that no matter who we are, where we are, or what we have, there will come a time when we will be faced with a situation in which our resources will prove to be an inadequate defense.

During these times, God wants to teach us that as soon as we acknowledge, through prayer, our insufficiency and His all-sufficiency, we are home free and victory is ours. Jehoshaphat teaches us what the wise man or woman does when faced with a seemingly insurmountable situation. He or she prays first and not last.

Another lesson gleaned from the story of Jehoshaphat is that when pressed by our enemies on every side, God wants us to come boldly to the throne of grace. But He also wants us to come quickly. Why do we wait so long to pray? It doesn't matter how many armies are coming against us, *"we are more than conquerors through Him who loved us"* (Romans 8:37). Someone has said that "Satan fighting against God is like a gnat fighting against an elephant."

It is usually fear that grips us and then paralyzes us to the point that we are even actually too afraid to ask God for what we want or need. But as Dr. Charles Stanley often says, "God is just sitting on ready, waiting for His children to call on Him in their time of need."

A scene from the story of the Prodigal Son demonstrates God's anticipation and eagerness to help His children. The story is also illustrative of the biblical principle that "When we're down to nothing, God is up to something." And since God, by His very nature is good, whatever He's up to has to be good, if not fantastic. The Prodigal Son has arrived at his father's compound and is first glimpsed by his father *"when he was yet a great way off."* The Bible says the father had compassion, broke out and ran to meet him, grabbed him, hugged him, fell on his neck and showered him with kisses (Luke 15:20).

The Prodigal Son is symbolic of all of us when we stray from the Father, His plan and purpose for our life. All we have to do is turn from our worldly ways, return to the Father's house and dwell amidst the lavish abundance of love, security and supply that can only be provided by our Heavenly Father.

Ruthlessness

It is high time that ruthlessness stood and took her bow. It is high time that we see her from God's perspective. It is high time that we see her as heaven sent and not hell bent. It is high time that we see the nugget of gold that lays nestled in her hair. It is high time that we pay homage to ruthlessness for all she is and all she will ever be: God sent and love meant—for all eternity.

We glean the meaning of most words from their ordinary usage in everyday conversation. As a child, there were times when my parents, grandmother, their friends and neighbors, and other close relatives considered their adult conversation suitable for our ears, if not for our vocal participation. In other words, we could sit quietly and listen, we just couldn't talk. I don't know about my brothers— they were usually outside playing ball—but I regarded these conversations as my after-school academy. I learned so much wisdom from listening to my parents and grandmother that I'll never be able to thank them enough!

During these conversations, I recall certain individuals as being referred to as ruthless. Not cruel or merciless, but ruthless. At least three such characters still stand out in my mind. The landlord who didn't miss a beat to have you evicted after you'd lost your job and could no longer pay the rent on time was said to be ruthless. The corner store merchant who charged you twice the price for the credit he extended to you when you didn't have the cash to buy bread and milk for your family was considered ruthless. The mother who abandoned her children when she would no longer tolerate the abuse by her husband—whether physical, verbal or mental— was regarded as ruthless.

Ruthlessness and ruthless both stem from the Hebrew root word ruth. The dictionary defines ruth as "compassion for the misery of another; sorrow for one's own faults." Ruthful is defined as "full of ruth: tender; full of sorrow." Ruthless and ruthlessness are defined as "having no ruth; merciless." The Hebrew origin of ruth is taken from the biblical character, Ruth, the "Moabite woman who accompanied Naomi to Bethlehem and became the ancestress of David."

(*Webster's New Collegiate Dictionary,* G. & C. Merriam Co.: Springfield, Massachusetts, 1977. p. 1015).

Based on my childhood definition of ruthless and ruthlessness, for many years as an adult, I excised the use of both words from my vocabulary. However, my parents and grandmother had also taught me to give people the benefit of the doubt; that is, to see them as made in the image and likeness of God; to treat them as I would want to be treated. I had never considered myself as subject to being at any level described as ruthless until a close family member referred to me as such. I was taken aback, if not shocked. "Who? Me? Ruthless? No way. Could it just be that an aspect of me was being revealed that I was unaware of? I embraced the suggestion, became quiet and began to pray for God's insight on the heels of this family member's observation of me.

It was at this time that I began to look closely at the definition of ruthlessness. I concluded that while this family member's observation might be accurate, their definition was inaccurate. What was needed was a new, contemporary definition of ruthlessness. If I considered myself ruthless, it was a ruthlessness that adheres to what I believe is a godly view of ruthlessness; a ruthlessness that, defined from God's perspective, is the ability to act mercilessly and without tenderness with ourselves, in the use of our limited amount of time in the earth, and in the pursuit, discovery and execution of our divine assignment.

We must be ruthless in showing no mercy and saying "no" to those who would steer us in directions that carry us away from the goals of our divine mission. Ruthlessness, from the godly perspective, is sifting the use of our precious time through the grid of God's divine intention for each moment of our day.

Ruthlessness demands that we see only what is God's will for the use of our time at any given moment. Ruthlessness is, at a critical level, denial of self and surrender to the Most High God. It is the unbroken, even obsession in the completion of God-given goals. It is the tough love and discipline exhibited by Anne Sullivan Macy in her molding and transformation of the great and remarkable Helen Keller from a blind and deaf child to a world renowned scholar and leader.

We must resolve to be ruthless in domestic matters, large and small. We must become impervious to dust around our house or apartment. We must decline routine conversations with family members that soak up our time when we are in the midst of meeting certain self-imposed deadlines in pursuit of our godly dreams. When we are working on a mission task, we must either shut the telephone off altogether or learn to ignore the ring. When you are satisfied with the use of a given block of time in your day, you may then check and review messages, including urgent calls that often prove to be urgent to the caller, but not necessarily urgent to you. Learning to be unavailable to those who would usurp the time God has given you to fulfill your unique mission will pay off in great future dividends.

During my first year in law school, ruthlessness offered herself to me as a dear friend. This was in the 70's and before the extensive telephone technology that we all take for granted today, including voice mail and caller I.D. With a 16 credit hour law school work load, a husband, 3 year old daughter, nine room Dutch Colonial house and German shepherd dog to care for, I had to choose between my former schedule of endless phone chats with friends and family, and the endless reading assignments for each of my law school classes.

During the week and on weekends, I would answer the phone and then spend fifteen minutes saying I had to go. Eventually, when I had homework—and I always had homework—I just unplugged the telephone to avoid hearing a ringing telephone that I didn't intend to answer. Of course, one or two of my friends said I no longer had time to talk. What they meant, but didn't say, was that I was being ruthless. While my close family members didn't drop me, they got used to being told that I was at the law library, so don't expect a return call.

Ruthlessness had not only become my dear friend, but bosom buddy who helped to get me through. She helped me to guard against frittering away my time. She reminded me that I must allow God to favor me in ways that would astound me. She was there to caution me of the great disappointment that would be mine if, at the end of my earthly journey, I looked back and realized that I had been woefully remiss in carrying out my God-given mission in the earth.

Does adherence to a practice and personal policy of ruthlessness mean that you never take time out to relax or to socialize with family and friends? Of course not. It just means that you are vigilant in the use of the precious and limited time you have been given. Catherine Marshall, in relating the wonderful story of the life of her husband, Peter Marshall, the former Senate Chaplain, shares with her readers how Peter always talked about being "under orders." There was never a day when Peter was not aware that God had given him life to accomplish certain tasks on behalf of the Master. (*A Man Called Peter*, McGraw-Hill Book Company, Inc.: New York, N.Y., 1951.)

To those who would deter us from our unique mission designed by our heavenly Father, ruthlessness responds, "...*I must be about my Father's business*" (Luke 2:49).

"The Very Hairs Of Your Head Are All Numbered"

God has made us for no other reason than to love us—and to love us unconditionally. He loves us when we're good and He loves us when we're bad. I am reminded of the lyrics from the Christmas carol, "*Santa Claus Is Coming To Town:*"

"He knows when we are sleeping.
He knows when we're awake.
He knows when we've been good or bad.
So be good for goodness sake!"

God knows us. He knows us in ways that no one else knows us. After all, He formed us in our mothers' wombs without any help from anyone else, including our mothers and fathers. God has shaped and molded us in such a fashion that, out of the billions of people in the world, our fingerprints are solely and uniquely ours. Because of my legal training and experience as a criminal defense counsel, the word "fingerprints," without any effort on my part, conjures up images of lock-ups, mug shots, court dockets and injustice too often visited upon the least of us.

I readily and unabashedly acknowledge the workings of my God-given natural mind. But thank God, on these occasions, I am grateful that I can move forward in the spirit of the Christ Mind that is also in me in the person of the Holy Spirit. It is with the Christ Mind that I am able to see beyond any man made restraints to the everlasting love, grace and mercy of the Lord Jesus Christ. It is He who has given me my own set of fingerprints as a testament to his marvelous goodness and glory that carries my soul "*somewhere over the rainbow, way up high*" to the foothills of heaven, the mercy seat of the Savior and the throne room of the Maker of heaven and earth and all that in them is.

God knows you so intimately that "*...the very hairs of your head are all numbered*" (Matthew 10:30). For many years, my understanding of this verse of scripture was not a complete one. However, one day I had the occasion to hear a preacher, whose name escapes me, explain that in this verse of Scripture, God is telling us that He not only knows the number of strands of hair of our head, but that He has so uniquely knit us together that each strand of hair of our head has its own number. So that God knows strand number 484 from strand number 4,417. Awesome!

What more does God have to say to prove His intimate knowledge of us? What more does He have to say to prove that we are His special masterpieces? What more does He have to say to prove that our uniqueness is designed to fit us for the special tasks that are ours alone. What more does He have to say to encourage our spiritual understanding that the world is waiting "to be ennobled by our fullest participation."

It is with the Christ Mind resident within me that I know that at the core of God's desire to love us unconditionally is His desire to have a personal and intimate relationship with us. Intimacy is, and always will be, characteristic of God's love for us. *Webster's New Collegiate Dictionary* defines *intimacy* as "the state of being intimate: familiarity. Whereas, *intimate* when used as an adjective is defined as follows: "intrinsic, essential; belonging to or characterizing one's deepest nature; marked by very close association, contact, or familiarity; marked by a warm friendship developing through long association; suggesting informal warmth or privacy; of a very personal or private nature."

While there can be intimacy without love; there can be no love without intimacy. Intimacy is commonly experienced in the absence of love. But genuine love cannot exist without the presence of real intimacy.

But getting back to love, and more specifically, God's unconditional love for us, at the end of the day, this is all that we have to know to successfully complete our sacred sojourn in the earth and to bear, with faith and hope, the weight of the personalized crosses that await us on our individual paths. To borrow wise insight from Dr. Raymond Charles Barker, the late Senior Pastor of the First Church of Religious Science of New York City, *"It is not what to do, but what to know."*

For if we know the truth of God's unconditional love for us, we are going to ultimately, if not initially, behave as beloved children of a loving Father who just happens to be sovereignly in control of every action and inaction in the world. I say ultimately, because our weak, human nature will cause us to get off track and even compromise our moral compass. We all have our seasons of prodigal adventures that in time lead us back to our heavenly Father who sits on ready, waiting and willing to bestow upon us the abundant life that we have been created to enjoy.

Wits' End Mall

*"They reel to and fro, and stagger
like a drunken man, and are at their
wit's end.
Then they cry unto the Lord in their
trouble, and he bringeth them out of
their distresses."*

Psalm 107:27-28

When you are at your wits' end, when you are stumped and "at a loss for a means of solving a problem," to quote the late Dr. Charles Raymond Barker, the issue is no longer "what to do, but what to know." The first thing to know is that Jesus has been waiting for you to come to your wits' end, so that His work, on your behalf, could begin.

Have you been roaming in Wits' End Mall lately? Is your heart troubled, and you don't know what to do, who to talk to or where to go? Have your family and friends deserted you, and you face this battle alone? Have you been battered, bloodied, bruised and abused? Are you simply exhausted from the vicious battle? Are your burdens stacked high and heavy, leaving you fatigued, weary and worn? Have you run out of words to pray—other than to ask God for strength for one more day?

Well, take heart my Friend. For there is no better place to be than at your wits' end. It is at your wits' end where God's power is shown; at your wits' end where your belief in God's faithfulness is born; at your wits' end where you trust God's heart to help you, even when you can't see His hand. It is at your wits' end where the Burden-Bearer stands—ready to demonstrate His determined will, purpose and plan. It is at Wits' End Mall where God proves His ways are far above man's.

The Holy Spirit that resides within us is more than capable of solving our problems, but only if we let Him. We arrive at our wits' end, not accidentally, but intentionally. We are there because we have tried everything we know. We have left no stone unturned in attempting to solve our problem and nothing has worked. We've found the world's remedies insufficient and inadequate. Band-aids are used to dress third degree burns.

For the child of God, and from God's perspective, there can be no better place than at your wits' end. By the time we come to our wits' end, we have had at least one good hand-to-hand combat with Satan. And while we are not down for the count, we have been battered, bruised and bloodied pretty badly.

Jesus sees our wits' end as the classroom of His sacred school. It is His opportunity to teach us the following eternal biblical truths:

>"…*the weapons of our warfare are not carnal, but mighty through God to the pulling down of strongholds*" (2 Corinthians 10:4);

>"…*He is the vine and we are the branches…that we can do nothing without Him*" (John 15:5);

>"… *heaven and earth shall pass away, but His word remains forever*" (Matthew 24:35);

>"…*if my people, which are called by my name, shall humble themselves, and pray, and seek my face, and turn from their wicked ways; then will I hear from heaven and will forgive their sin, and will heal their land*" (2 Chronicles 7:14);

>"…*if we shall commit our way unto the Lord, and trust also in Him, He will bring our desires to pass*" (Psalm 37:5); and

>"…*we are more than conquerors through Him that loved us*" (Romans 8:37).

And so the next time you find yourself at your wits' end—no matter how relentless the pain and pressure—see it as a time of remembrance of all the promises of God and the spiritual lessons that Jesus shed His precious blood to teach us.

See your Wits' End Mall as a holy place; a time not to roam, but to stand and stay on bended knees on the inside; and to surrender to His will, His way and His time. Resolve to use your wits' end experience as a time when you tell the Father to do with you as He wills; a time when you are willing to allow the Father to do with you as He pleases; a time of holy communion when you are willing to let God have His way with you; a sacred time when—whether He crushes you, exalts you or puts you on the shelf—your spirit and soul will say "Yes, Lord."

"Hell Works The Hardest On God's Saints"

Have you ever looked around and wondered why the people who appear to do the right thing and treat people right seem, almost without exception, to encounter the most hell?

I am somewhat embarrassed to admit that it has taken me almost a lifetime to understand the lesson the Holy Spirit has been teaching me all along. The lesson is eloquently taught by Christian author L.B. Cowman when she astutely observes that "*...Hell works the hardest on God's saints. The most worthy souls will be tested with the most pressure and the highest heat, but heaven will not desert them.*" (Op. Cit., p. 197).

Saints are not perfect people. They run the race. They make mistakes. They fall down, skin their knee caps, and bruise their elbows. They pick themselves up, brush themselves off and get back on their path. They have lapses in which they gossip, envy and covet what is their neighbor's. They have falling-outs with God. They utter expletives when under pressure—and immediately ask God to forgive them. There are times when they tell God where to go, and offer to buy His ticket to get Him there. They have been known to question the wisdom of God's plan and purpose in the circumstances that confront them.

But if there is one characteristic, above all others, that identifies a saint, it is his or her faithful commitment to the divine perspective; the perspective that contemplates all circumstances from God's point of view; a perspective that sees everything as either ordained by God, or permitted by God, for His ultimate glory and their ultimate gain.

The Bible assures us that, if we are followers of Christ, we shall endure hardship, pain, difficulty and trial. We shall also be persecuted and all manner of evil shall be committed against us. However, our job is to remember that "*Our struggle is not against flesh and blood, but against the rulers, against the authorities...and against the spiritual forces of evil in the heavenly realms*" (Ephesians 6:12). "Even the fact that we face a trial proves there is something very precious to our Lord in us, or else He would not spend so much time and energy on us" (Cowman, Op. Cit., p. 77).

One of the mighty truths of the Gospel is that the closer we are to the cross, the closer we are to the resurrection. When Satan hovered around Christ in the Garden of Gethsemane, it would be just a matter of three days before Jesus would be resurrected, arise and ascend to heaven. There He would sit at the right hand of God, the Father, interceding on behalf of every child of God.

And so dear Friend, if, as you read these words, you are experiencing a difficult hardship or trial; remember that God is with you in the circumstance. He's in absolute control of every aspect of the circumstance. He is working out the total circumstances for His glory and your greatest good, *provided* you trust Him to know what is best for you, and yield completely to His way of working in your life.

The Devil comes to steal, kill and destroy. The child of God is his prime target of choice. A child of God is alive in Christ; is blessed according to the riches that are in Christ Jesus; has access to all the riches that are in heaven; and possesses a body that is the temple of the Holy Spirit.

The next time hell seems to be working particularly hard on you, rejoice and give thanks unto God that apparently the Devil sees that there is something so precious about you that he has set out to steal, kill or destroy your godly witness and your divine assignment in the earth. Moreover, he has set out to obliterate you and the godly resource that you represent to the Body of Christ and to the world at large.

A saint is a servant of God, and so is Satan. He just needs to be reminded of that fact by the saint's attitude, conduct, conversation and confession. He can do no more than he is permitted to do by God. All of Satan's activities and the activities of those whom he dominates are within the parameters set by God. Therefore, we do not have to fear Satan. Rather, we can look him squarely in the face and be assured that he can do no more than God permits him to do, because Satan is under orders, too.

Satan's Abuse Precedes God's Great Use

When several of the Disciples asked Jesus if they could sit with Him at the right hand of the Father, Jesus answered by asking if they could drink from the bitter cup that He drank from. L.B. Cowman does not mince words when she shares with her readers her view of the importance of brokenness in the life of the believer that is to be used mightily by the Lord: "God never uses anyone to a great degree until He breaks the person completely" (Op. Cit., p. 41).

How often have we heard someone say they want to be used greatly by the Lord? However, upon close examination of their life, we are able to observe that they have used every means within their power to escape the crucibles that have been placed along their path. These painful experiences have been custom-designed by God to prepare us to be used greatly by God. They are our spiritual training grounds, our boot camps, if you will, to toughen us up and get us ready for the spiritual warfare that awaits us in every test and trial.

God knows what it will take to put us right in the middle of the arena of life. He knows what it will take to get us off the bench and out of the bleachers. It might be the loss of a job. It might be a spousal separation or divorce. It might be a health challenge or financial setback. Whatever the personal trauma, God has already planned to use it to position you just where He wants to use you to bring light to some darkened area of the world, and in so doing bring Him honor and glory.

If we are to be used greatly by God, we must be willing to take up our cross daily, in whatever shape it takes, and follow Him. We must be willing to let others choose the nails that shall pierce our hands and feet. By God's grace, we must surrender to letting others determine the contents of the bitter cup from which we shall drink. Sometimes the pain will be tolerable and sometimes not. And when it is excruciatingly intolerable, when we can bear it no more, we will often find ourselves crying out to the Father, "Why, Lord?" "Why me?" "Why this?" "Why now?"

Life is the combination of the bitter and the sweet, the sunshine and the rain, joy and sadness, pleasure and pain. In the midst of our deepest pain, God wants us to surrender to His Lordship. His Lordship is comprised of His omnipotence, His omnipresence and His omniscience. We have been emotionally structured to use our most hurtful experiences as opportunities that build our resolve; and strengthen our character needed to accomplish our divine assignment.

Our tests and trials are the seeds that the Holy Spirit uses to increase our wisdom and knowledge of the ways of the Father. Our assumption of a Divine perspective of the circumstances of life gives us a spiritual dexterity that enables us to handle the difficulties and hardships of life with calm confidence and quiet assurance amidst the howling winds and rains that can be counted on to batter and bruise our spirits as the depth of our faith is tested and tried.

God is calling each one of us to *persist past the point of pain* of our circumstances. And L.B. Cowman reminds us that: *"Evil never surrenders its grasp without a tremendous fight..."* (Op. Cit., p. 98). When we're in the deepest purgatory, we must resolve to see Jesus right in the middle of the mix, waiting for us with His arms outstretched. God wants us to kneel beneath our old rugged cross. He wants us to carry it, without mumbling a word, to Jesus—again and again.

When we have resigned to being finally entombed by our circumstances, we shall look up one day and realize that the stone has been rolled away, the third day has arrived and we have been transformed and resurrected into a new life with Christ Jesus. To our surprise, we realize that we are now walking along the road to Emmaus, telling our friends, and all those who care to listen, what the Lord has done for us.

Perhaps we are now ready to be used by God, according to His magnificent plan and purpose.

Enrollment In The Class of Hard Times

Hard times are as certain to come to us, as are good times. Hard times challenge us to hunker down and then grow up in the ways of the Lord. As students, and by God's grace, we are enrolled in this classroom called life. We are to master life's lessons by studying the Word of God and then applying the biblical principles to our every day tasks and challenges, however insufferable.

It is the hard times, times of pain and suffering, times of loss and betrayal, times of financial strain and marital stress that teach us the most valuable lessons. Therefore, admonishes author L.B. Cowman, *"When hard times come, be a student, not a victim."* Hard times, in and of themselves, do not make us better, wiser and stronger. Rather, it is our view of hard times from God's perspective. God allows nothing in our lives that is not intended to bless us in a mighty way.

Hard times teach us at least four lessons that enable us to navigate all through the deep waters that we shall, from time to time, encounter. The first lesson is that God is a good God. Because it is His nature to be good, He can't be anything but good. He is not a God who is good on Monday, but not good on Tuesday. He is not good in good times, but not good in hard times. No, God is good all the time.

The second lesson is that God is faithful. He keeps His promises to the letter of His word; dotting all His i's and crossing all His t's. His promises are made to last throughout all eternity.

As a student of hard times, the third lesson that we are afforded the opportunity to learn is the lesson set forth poetically in Psalm 46: *"God is our refuge and strength, a very present help in trouble."*

The lesson that times of trouble teach us is that it is God, and not our friends or even family members, which can always be counted on to be the present help we need in times of trouble. Although much divine help comes through the channel of human help, human help is impotent outside of the will, grace and mercy of the Father. But the Father's help is always a help that is a very present help in times of trouble. In other words, the help is so specific and so timely that it cannot be mistaken as anything but God.

The fourth and final lesson that hard times teach us is that in the classroom of our hard times, God proves Himself to be El Shaddai, the God who is more than enough for any experience of hard times (John 14:13). As students of the Master Teacher and Most High God, we are blessed and highly favored to learn, first hand, that our God is a God who is more than enough. He is a God who has promised that if He doesn't have what we need, He'll make it for us!

When we resolve to remain steadfast in the midst of hard times, pain and persecution, we learn to see hard times as high times of opportunity for God to demonstrate His power, love and sovereignty over all.

Disappointment Is His Appointment

God knows no disappointment. There is no disappointment in Spirit. There is only God's will, God's design, God's plan and God's purpose.

Webster's Ninth New Collegiate Dictionary (Springfield, Massachusetts: Merriam-Webster Inc., 1984) defines disappointment as follows: "The act or an instance of disappointing." Whereas it defines the verb "disappoint" in this manner: "to fail to meet the expectation or hope of." It also gives the root word as taken from the French word "desapointier: *des*-dis- + *apointier* to arrange." On the other hand, the prefix "dis" is defined as "do the opposite of." I've never been so surprised to discover the dictionary meaning, along with the root word, for "disappointment." I don't ever recall researching the origin of its meaning.

As the dictionary meaning of disappointment demonstrates, even in the midst of our disappointment, God is arranging our life, and the lives of our loved ones, according to His sacred and immutable plan and purpose. And often God's plan is the opposite of our plan in a given situation. As one writer has aptly stated, "If you want to make God laugh, tell Him your plans."

In Jeremiah 29:11 (LB), the Word from the Lord to be considered when we are making plans of any sort: *For I know the plans I have for you, says the Lord. They are plans for good...to give you a future and a hope.* From the Father's perspective, all disappointment is His appointment, His eternal arrangement of the circumstances of our lives.

It is our heavenly Father who specializes in the unconditional love of His children that sends the circumstances that we refer to as disappointment. And while it is not the nature of God to create the cacophony of cares that we interpret as disappointment, we can be certain that He is always there orchestrating the combination of circumstances that often appear, from our human perspective, as confusing, if not chaotic.

What peace and contentment we experience when we see disappointment, without exception, as His appointment. What joy divine is ours when we embrace all disappointment as His appointment. What exquisite peace is ours when we finally realize that it can never be anything else.

God loves us too much to allow us to experience pain that is not productive. Disappointment should say to us, "persist past the point of pain" to the secret place where God shows you His plan and purpose for the pain in your life. In the words of C.A. Fox, "The disappointments of life are simply the hidden appointments of love."

"Wear It As A Loose Garment"

I shall never be able to thank my grandmother, Rosa Lee Bradley Washington Terry, enough for teaching me that no matter what problem or trouble I am facing, I must always remember to "Wear it as a loose garment."

A loose garment wears easily and flows freely. It does not pinch or chafe. You don't feel stifled as you move from place to place. It allows the body to relax no matter what the occasion or circumstance. It promotes its own cooling system for the benefit of the wearer, as the air blows in balanced breezes in response to the movement of the garment.

A loose garment allows its wearer to breathe easily, without having to wait to inhale or exhale. It does not reveal either bumps or curves, but maintains, undisclosed, the sacred integrity of its wearer; privileged to clothe the body that is the temple of the Holy Ghost.

After all these many years, I can still hear Mama say, *"Problems are a part of life. Ain't no use trying to avoid them. But you can handle them in such a way that God will bring you out more than conquered. And the way to do that is to just wear your problems as a loose garment."* This, in essence, is a restatement of "Mama's Theology of the Loose Garment."

Wearing our problems as a loose garment, in and of itself, is not difficult. What causes the strain and stress of any kind of trouble that besets us is that we refuse to see the trouble or hardship as having come through God's hands long before it reaches us. He, and He alone, has uniquely designed and tailored our problems, without exception, to develop us into the godly people that can make a needed difference in the world. God has given the nod and green light to every situation, however troubling, that we face.

Our Father is the Great Designer, the Incomparable Architect, and Eternal Engineer of this magnificent and marvelous universe. He is the wonderful counselor and mighty advocate to all who call upon Him in their time of need for help of any kind, at any time.

When we are able to wear our tests and trials as a loose garment that has been washed in the blood of Jesus, we testify to an unbelieving and fallen world that He is the Way, the Truth and the Life; and that no man or woman comes to the Father but by Him.

The Keys to Victory Over Our Adversaries

If you are a follower of Christ, and committed to allowing the Word of God to discipline and determine your conversation, conduct and character, you will eventually come under severe and satanic attack. These times must not mystify nor stump you. We live in a fallen world. Evil, in every imaginable design and degree, abounds, touches and concerns everyone.

In the Epistle of James, we are clearly instructed as to what should be the right response and conduct of a servant of God and of the Lord Jesus Christ:

> *"My brethren, count it all joy*
> *when ye fall into divers temptations;*
> *Knowing this, that the trying of*
> *your faith worketh patience.*
> *But let patience have her perfect*
> *work, that ye may be perfect and*
> *entire, wanting nothing."*

James 1: 2-4

Notice that James doesn't say "if" you fall into divers temptations. He says "when." In other words, it's a given that you shall come under satanic attack. You can count on it. You will be attacked— repeatedly, viciously, and relentlessly. Perhaps you are experiencing some form of attack at the present time. If you have recently come through some form of attack, then the previously cited biblical instruction of James may have more meaning for you.

James promises us that the reward of standing firm, and not quitting and running, when we're under attack, is *"that we may be perfect and entire, wanting nothing."* In other words, if, when we're attacked, we adopt an attitude of joy, because, like our brother Job, we know that our Redeemer lives and therefore, we know that He is calling all the shots, no matter how fierce and relentless the battle, what is there to fear or worry about?

I particularly cherish a description of the "Keys to Victory" for the believer under attack, as taught by Dr. Charles F. Stanley in one of his many wonderful teachings that I have been privileged and blessed by God to hear. Dr. Stanley instructed that when we come under attack, either as a result of our own disobedience, or due to an attack by Satan, or due to the permissive will of God, we shall obtain the victory over any assault on our person or whatever we hold dear, if we shall utilize the following five keys to victory: 1) Become quiet; 2) Stay calm; 3) Don't retaliate; 4) Step back; and 5) Watch God work.

There can be no lasting victory over our circumstances without the acknowledgement of the sovereignty of God and the renouncement of Satan and all his works. Moreover, there must be deference and obedience to God's will, plan and purpose in every situation. This is why our brother, James, admonishes us to let our faith be tried so that it will produce the patience that is needed to wait on God for the perfect outworking of His will in our life. If we will follow James' instruction, God will then be able to use us in any way that He sees fit. Your reward will be blessings beyond measure.

"Broken Focus"

"And Peter answered him and said, Lord, if it be thou, bid me come unto thee on the water.

And he said, Come. And when Peter was come down out of the ship, he walked on the water, to go to Jesus.

*But when he saw **the wind boisterous**, he was afraid; and beginning to sink, he cried, saying Lord, save me.*

And immediately Jesus stretched forth his hand, and caught him, and said unto him, O thou of little faith, wherefore didst thou doubt?"

Matthew 14:28-31

Nothing defeats our dreams, sinks our ships and sabotages our success, in carrying out our divine assignment, as does broken focus. I was first introduced to the spiritual principle of broken focus by Dr. Mike Murdock. Broken focus is taking our eyes off Jesus, after He has told us to "come." Here, in the Gospel of Matthew, we find Peter with his eyes fixed on Jesus. Moreover, we find Peter bold enough and brave enough to get out of the boat and walk on the water to meet Jesus, *after* Jesus told him to "come." But Peter let the boisterous wind frighten him, and his fear caused him to begin to sink. As one astute observer has remarked, "Once Peter got out of the boat, the waves (and wind) were none of his business."

Peter's failure to continue to walk on the water was attributed to his broken focus. He took his eyes off Christ. Peter began to look at the winds and the waves and feared that he would drown. In that one moment of broken focus on Jesus, Peter forgot that he had been focused on the One who made the wind and waves and controlled their force and power.

There are so many spiritual truths and lessons that we can glean from this story. The first is that, as children of God, we *can* walk on water. At first blush, that might seem preposterous, but it's true. If Jesus tells us to come to Him, and coming to Him means walking on water, then we must know, without qualification or reservation, that we *can* walk on water. To question this truth is to second guess the Son of God, our Savior and the Sovereign of the universe.

Have you ever heard Jesus tell you to "come" to Him, and you faithfully obeyed? You climb out of your boat and begin to walk on the water. But then in an instant, you are distracted by a boisterous wind. Your attention and focus is now on the boisterous wind. You become consumed with the wind and its ability to keep you from walking on the water. You no longer see Jesus. You no longer see His power, protection, peace and prosperity. You see only the boisterous wind and your inevitable end. You have, in the twinkling of an eye, become the victim of broken focus. And tragically, right in the presence of Omnipotence, you begin to sink.

When we step out of our boats and respond to Jesus' calling on our life, we must keep our focus on Him at all times. The reason most of us fail to walk on the water to meet Jesus is because, like Peter, we take our eyes off Jesus and put our focus on the boisterous wind and waves. The boisterous wind and waves are all those things in the world that distract us from our calling. Typically, the boisterous wind is distracting, if not outright toxic, personal relationships. Or it could be the boisterous wind of lack of money; sickness and disease; seasons of unemployment; disappointment and depression; some hardship, pain, trial or persecution; and loss of any kind. These are times when Jesus is testing our faith. Do we trust Him to handle the boisterous wind and waves or not?

You are in your senior year of high school and your dream has always been to further your formal education by achieving a college degree. In your spirit, you feel that Jesus is telling you to "come;" to walk on the water to meet Him. However, your parents tell you they have no money to send you to college; you need to just plan on getting a job when you finish school.

You must see this discouragement as nothing more than a boisterous wind and keep your focus on Jesus. Jesus has all the supply that you will need to finish high school. He has the college application fees that you will need. He has the tuition, room, board, scholarships and grants that you will need. He has the travel costs that you will need. He has the money for your text books, computers and materials. In other words, He has everything that you will need, if

He has told you to "come." And you must never forget that He has promised that, as El Shaddai, "*...if he doesn't have what you need, he'll make it for you*" (John 14:13).

Classic is Dr. Mike Murdock's teaching on broken focus found in his *Seeds of Wisdom on Your Assignment* (The Wisdom Center: Fort Worth, TX, 2001, p. 24). It is certainly worth repeating here. On the issue of the spiritual principle of broken focus, Dr. Murdock masterfully instructs us as follows:

"The only reason men fail is broken focus...You will only succeed when your assignment becomes an obsession...

The Apostle Paul was obsessed with his assignment....

It explains his remarkable victories over enemies, adversaries and even friends who misunderstood him...Be ruthless in refusing any responsibilities unrelated to your assignment.

Prepare for uncommon adversity. Satan dreads the completion of your assignment. Each act of obedience can destroy a thousand satanic plans and desires...Fight for your focus...Battle hard. Build walls that guarantee your concentration...

Ignore the jeers, laughter and criticism that you are 'obsessed.'...

Only the obsessed succeed."

Principalities and Powers

We are all faced with having to sometimes interact with people who would just as easily tell an untruth as they would the truth. Every now and then, it becomes our lot to cross the path of deceptive, difficult, desperate, dangerous, and by any standard, even demonic individuals. Many fellow travelers walk among us in darkness, unaware of the light of Jesus Christ, or, having been shown the light, prefer the darkness over the light.

When we are engaged in any endeavor and find ourselves face to face with satanic operatives, we must see them for what they are—principalities and powers; mere pawns in Satan's palm; agents of the evil one. In Ephesians 6:12, we are told, *"For we wrestle not against flesh and blood, but against principalities, against powers, against the rulers of the darkness of this world, against spiritual wickedness in high places."*

Our stance against the Devil's designees, if it is to be effective, must be comprised of never ceasing prayer and meditation on the Word of God. This must be followed by our sincere commitment to live holy—not perfectly—but holy. Acrostically, HOLY simply means "having our lives yielded."

No matter the nature of our warfare with evil, Paul astutely instructs us in 2 Corinthians 10:4: *"For the weapons of our warfare are not carnal, but mighty through God to the pulling down of strong holds."* They, of course, are the weapons outlined in the sixth chapter of the Book of Ephesians. They are the following: *the helmet of salvation, the breastplate of righteousness, the shield of faith, the girdle of truth, the shoes of the gospel of peace, and the sword of the Spirit.*

When others are being used by the enemy in spiritual warfare, they show themselves in their conduct, conversation and confession as unrepentant sinners who have fallen far short of the glory of God.

Principalities and powers, however potent, will forever submit to the plan and purpose of the Almighty, as well as to the prayers and petitions of the saints of God.

"You Are Too Gifted To Be Broke"

However circuitous, or not so circuitous, the path that finds you, a child of God, broke, take heed to the marvelous words of Bishop Noel Jones, Founder of Noel Jones Ministries, and know that "*You are too gifted to be broke.*" This is the time to follow in the footsteps of the Prodigal Son and rise up and declare for the entire world to hear: "I'm too gifted, beloved and beautiful to be backed up and broke."

When you fail to use your unique, God-given gifts and talents, or you use them in a manner that doesn't fit God's plan and purpose for your life; you become a choked channel for the cornucopia of blessings that the Lord desires to give you. When you are not using your gifts and talents at all, or you are using them in the wrong way, you are out of God's will for your life. And when we're out of God's will for our life, we are certain to experience varying degrees of being broke.

Disobedience to God's instruction in the use of our divine gifts and talents leads to the pain and humiliation of being broke. *Webster's Ninth New Collegiate Dictionary* defines the word "broke" in one word: "penniless." And, of course, this is the condition we experience when we are broke. We are penniless. We are usually, at a critical time, virtually bereft of all financial resources. Being broke is not a pretty place to be. It is not a place where we want to tarry too long. And yet many of us have been there, at one time or another.

However, from God's viewpoint, the condition of being broke is a sacred place. It is a place where the Master Potter, the One who has formed, molded and made us expressly for His divine use, focuses our attention on Him, His plan and purpose for our life.

Your individual gifts and talents come to you sacredly sealed in God's anointing.

They precede your assignment. Your gifts and talents have been given to you by God and not by man. They are foundational to all that you do in His name and for His Glory.

Long before you were born, you were empowered by the Father to uniquely express your gifts and talents in a manner as no one else can. God has already sanctioned and approved the godly expression of your gifts and talents. Very simply, this is referred to as the anointing. It is because of the anointing that what you do best and, seemingly without effort; others attempting to do the same thing, struggle along producing what at first appears to be fruit, but upon closer inspection, turns out to be only leaves.

It is a slap in the face of the Master to worry or wonder about what people will say about the use of your gifts in some, as yet, unexpressed manner. He has made you and He has need of you. Therefore, you don't need to spend time focused on people. He has already delivered you from people! You must commit to being about His business. And *His business is the express business.* You must give over to God other people's opinions, opposition or lack of support for the fullest expression of your God-given gift. He is controlling it all, anyway.

As followers of Christ, we must be ever mindful of the creative imperative that the Father has placed on our life. Similarly, we must, through never-ceasing prayer, guard against the myriad distractions and deceptions that militate against the production of our special fruit.

In the story of the fig tree found in Matthew 21:18-19, we are told that because the fig tree was remiss in its divine purpose, Jesus ordered the disciples to cut it down. When it comes to fruit inspection of our life, many of us are very much like the fig tree. We are producing an abundance of leaves, but no fruit. We look good producing leaves, but leaf production is not our mission; fruit production is our assignment. Therefore, we must be ever vigilant and committed to answering the call of the creative imperative on our life, in season and out of season.

It is our duty to stand ever ready and in continual preparation for unannounced fruit inspections by the Holy Ghost. For while "*we know neither the day nor the hour when He shall appear,*" we want to be like Him in letting the Father have His way in our life. No obedient child of God has to fear being cut down or put on the shelf by the Father, as discipline for our failure or refusal to carry out our divine assignment.

The message of the story of the fig tree is clear and unequivocal. If we rebelliously buck God's will, plan and purpose for our life; we might as well prepare to be cut down in one way or another. Or, the Father might decide to simply put us on the shelf until we are willing to humbly surrender to His loving call on our life, sweetly whispered in our inner ear. If you have not heard the call, perhaps it is because you have been too busy to slow down, be still and listen to the still small voice.

Almost without exception, when we're broke, we're not using our God-given gifts at all, or we're not using them to our maximum potential. It is the Father's signal of His disapproval, if not displeasure, with His child when He permits the condition of being broke. Whereas, God sees to it that untold spiritual and material success results from the proper use of our unique gifts and talents. Therefore, our perpetual prosperity is inextricably tied to our cultivation of the unique talents that have been given to each individual by the Father.

As children, many of us were taught that we could be whatever we wanted to be. This is partially true and partially false. If what we aspire to be falls outside of God's will, purpose and plan for our life, we shall achieve our life's work at the ultimate high price of death to our soul, death to our peace of mind, death to our personal integrity, self-respect and self–esteem. We can, for years, and in great leaf production, remain on jobs and in professions, carrying out fruitless assignments that were never ours to begin with.

We rationalize the prostitution of our God-given talents by saying that we needed money to pay the rent, the credit cards, the kids' tuition, the car note and on and on. But our God is a providing God. It has been said that if He gives us a vision, He will also give the provision to carry out the vision. God wants us to relate to Him based on His unconditional love for us; and His ability to do all things well and abundantly above all that we could ever ask or imagine.

The Devil wants us to believe that our gift is not worth developing, and if developed, will be of little use to us. But the Holy Scriptures teach us that *"A man's gift maketh room for him, and bringeth him before great men"* (Proverbs 18:16). Our primary task then is to rely on this promise of God, and go for it. Why, moreover, would God give us special talents and then not support us in our use of these talents? We can always count on God to support our efforts. God is one thing above all else— He is faithful.

Three things God will not support. He will not support our disobedience; He will not support our sinful indulgences; and He will not support our passivity. Scarcity and poverty are the results of failing to use our God-given talents and gifts according to God's plan for our life.

And if your divine assignment seems overwhelming at times, stop in the midst of your work, get down on your knees, bow your head and humbly remind the Father that it is He, and not you, that does the work. Moreover, remind Him that it is His work, and not your work, that you do.

Finally, remind Him that, without Him, "*you can do (absolutely) nothing*" (John 15:5). But with Him, "*you can do all things*" that He has planned and purposed through the power of the Holy Spirit that is resident within you (Philippians 4:13). Then step back and watch, to your amazement, how He supplies all your needs for the cultivation and implementation of your divine gifts "*according to His riches in glory by Christ Jesus*" (Philippians 4:19).

Ask

Ask. For help of any kind. *Ask.* For the healing of your heart. *Ask.* For your divine employment. *Ask.* For your right companion. *Ask.* For favor in the marketplace. *Ask.* For friends that sticketh closer than a brother. *Ask.* For a needed parking space. *Ask.* For needed supply — pressed down, shaken together, full to the brim and running over. *Ask.* For nothing less than a miracle, if a miracle is what you need. *Ask.* For your heart's deepest desire.

The Scriptures challenge us to *Ask* the Father for whatever we need, whenever we need it. Nevertheless, we fail to ask, even when our need is great to overwhelming. Is it because we are afraid of being turned down? Is it because we consider ourselves among the so-called little people whose requests are just not that important? Or are we simply unwilling to endure the timing required for our prayer seeds to take root, and sprout into the manifested fruit of answered prayer.

When we go to God in prayer with a request, do we also go with unwavering resolve to wait for His answer? Are we committed to wait whatever time it takes? Will we remain steadfast and faithful to the Father through the weeks, months and years that might be required in His work behind the scenes and underground? Will we remember to pause occasionally and consider that "it takes time for God to color a rose?"

In Matthew 7:11, Jesus reasons with us on the importance of asking for the Father's help: "*If ye then, being evil, know how to give good gifts unto your children, how much more shall your Father which is in heaven give good things to them that ask him?*" And in Psalm 68:19, David sings praises to God for blessings that exceed our need and request: "*Blessed be the Lord, who daily loadeth us with benefits, even the God of our salvation.*" Further, in Jeremiah 31:3, God's word assures us "*I have loved you with an everlasting love.*" And in 2 Corinthians 11:2, mindful of the world's competing attractions for the time and attention of His beloved, God says, "*For I am jealous over you with godly jealousy.*"

God invites us to come boldly to the throne of grace where we can receive grace and mercy in our time of need. But we cannot come boldly to the Father for the fulfillment of our needs if we are not willing to pray. It is prayer that is the prelude to the Father's fulfillment and supply of every need, every hour. But we must pray to pray. We must, at all times and in all places, commune with the Father. Prayer is the running dialogue that we maintain with the Master of the universe. It is what Paul meant when he said we are to pray in season and out of season; in the shower and in the supermarket; in the car and on the metro; in the library and in the lavatory; in the bedroom and in the kitchen.

We must not only ask God. We must ask God first and not last. Tell God your need, even though He already knows. Tell Him that you pledge to surrender to His plan, His time and His manner in the fulfillment of your need. Prepare to move your feet. Then wait and watch God work. You will be astounded at the unique and magnificent ways in which God will answer your prayer.

God has promised that if we come to Him with a specific request that He doesn't have, He'll right then and there make it for us (John 14:13).

It doesn't get any better than that!

In The Meantime Can Be A Mean time

Countless believers today have had a spiritual experience in their early life similar to that of Joseph, recounted in the Bible's thirty-seventh chapter of the Book of Genesis. In Joseph's teen years, God revealed his future earthly assignment. God showed Joseph in two dreams that he would be exalted over his brothers and their father, Jacob.

But in the meantime, Joseph would experience a mean time.

Joseph made the innocent mistake of telling his brothers of his dreams. Shortly thereafter, his brothers concocted a wicked plot to kill Joseph. His brother, Reuben, thinking of the utter grief Joseph's death would cause their father, persuaded his brothers to instead put Joseph in a pit.

Motivated by greed, they sold Joseph to Ishmaelite merchantmen for twenty pieces of silver. Joseph was then carried off to Egypt to be sold again as a slave. The brothers later tricked their father into believing that Joseph had been devoured by an evil beast when they showed their father Joseph's blood stained coat.

Even while being sold at auction as a slave, Joseph stood proudly and held his head high. He was certain that God would not forsake him. Although made a prisoner when he refused to commit adultery and was falsely accused, he remained patient and faithful to his trust in God.

God had so brilliantly arranged the circumstances in Joseph's life. It was through Joseph's God-given talent of interpreting dreams that Joseph was able to perform the special service of interpreting Pharaoh's dreams. Pharaoh was able to prepare for the seven years of famine that would follow the seven years of plenty. As a reward to Joseph, Pharaoh made Joseph a ruler over all of Egypt.

Through the thirteen years of wrongful imprisonment, Joseph had suffered immeasurably. However, Joseph had used the long and lonely years to forgive his brothers for their unspeakable, wicked deed.

Joseph had come to realize, through faith in God and his sovereignty, that it was God who had brought him to Egypt to carry out his assignment and to fulfill the plan and purpose that God had ordained for his life. Joseph had suffered deeply, however God was about to use him greatly.

Having endured the pit and prison, Joseph finally arrived in the palace from where he governed as ruler over all of Egypt.

Joseph's brothers had been mere putty in God's hands, no matter the depth of their evil acts. Therefore, when Joseph confronted his brothers, unable to hold back tears, he revealed his true identity. *"...I am Joseph, your brother; whom ye sold into Egypt"*(Genesis 45:4). Seeing the fear and shame on their faces, Joseph attempted to calm their fears. *"Now therefore, be not grieved nor angry with yourselves that ye sold me hither, for God did send me before you to preserve life"* (Genesis 45:5).

Joseph's words of consolation to his brothers centered on his awareness that it was God, and not they, who had engineered the circumstances of his life. Said Joseph to his brothers, *"What you intended for evil, God intended for good"* (Genesis 50:20). Joseph had learned that nothing is outside of the mighty control of the Father. And He uses even the actions of the wickedest of men to serve Him.

Joseph, sold into slavery at 17, lived to be 110 years old. That means Joseph enjoyed 80 years of fabulous living and 13 years of imprisonment. I am sure that Joseph would agree that his good days far outweighed and outnumbered his bad days.

And so the next time your "in the meantime" is by all measure a particularly mean time, don't be discouraged, but take heart. Our job is to keep our focus on God and the future He has promised us. God can be counted on to keep His promises. He will deliver. He is a man that does not, cannot lie.

"Where Were You When I Laid the Earth's Foundation?"

"Where were you when I laid the earth's foundation?" (Job 38:4 NIV). This is one of the piercing questions that God asked Job when Job engaged in questioning God about the great and dire misery that played out in sickness, loss, catastrophe, tragedy and deep suffering that God allowed Satan to bring into his life.

The other piercing question posed by God to Job was *"Have you ever given orders to the morning; and caused the dawn to take its place?"* (Job 38:12 NIV). God was in effect saying to Job "Until you have reached the level of my omnipotence, omniscience and omnipresence, you are without standing to question my actions in governance of the universe — period."

Job is every man and woman. We don't hesitate to question what God is up to and whether He really knows what He is doing. Many times our power to carry out our divine assignment is diminished by our second-guessing God regarding the hardship, trial and difficulty He allows to come into our life. Moreover, we get mired in the quicksand of trying to persuade God that our plan and purpose is superior to His. This stance results in a myriad of unfruitful and unproductive personal predicaments.

Instead of using our precious time to discern God's will for the use of our unique skills and talents, we sit around making feeble attempts to pick apart the plan of God. It is later that we realize that God's plan is impervious to any plan of man.

Put down your picks and hacksaws. Take up the sword of the Holy Spirit (the Word of God) and the shield of faith. You shall then be empowered to deflect all of the fiery darts of the evil one.

In one question to Job, God framed the core issue of every human experience from now until eternity. It is the issue of divine will versus human will. Actually, what Job finally came to understand is that there can be no contest or competition between divine will and human will. The very nature of human will mandates that it yield to divine will. Human will, in every instance, will be preempted by divine will. If this were not so, then God would not be sovereign.

Whenever and however human will stands up, it must ultimately bow to divine will. And the reason it must bow is because it will never be able to answer unequivocally, and without qualification, the question, *"Where were you when I laid the earth's foundation?"*

Give Yourself the Gift of Forgiveness

In January of 2005, world leaders and hundreds of concentration camp survivors assembled in Oswiecim, Poland to mark the 60th anniversary of the liberation of the Nazi death camp at Auschwitz-Birkenau.

It was reported that when Soviet troops liberated the camp, they discovered a 10-year-old girl named Eva, a victim of the medical experiments conducted by Josef Mengele, the head physician at Auschwitz.

Today she is Eva Mozes Kor. She is married and lives in the Midwest. While she has traveled to the camp several times over the past two decades to celebrate her survival and to make sure others remember what happened, the newspaper account of how she now perceives this entire nightmarish experience is a lesson for all mankind in the redemptive power of suffering and forgiveness:

"'I know most people won't understand this,'
she said, clutching a black-and-white photograph
taken by a Soviet soldier that shows her on
liberation day standing inside a barbed wire enclosure.
'But I have forgiven the Nazis.
I have forgiven Mengele.
I have forgiven everybody.
I no longer carry the burden of pain.
I have given myself the gift of forgiveness"
(*The Washington Post*, January, 2005).

Most of us have been spared, by the grace of God, the horror of being incarcerated in a Nazi death camp. However, there are still people in our lives that we consider to have harmed us in some way. We need to follow the incredible example of Eva Moses Kor and forgive those who have despitefully used us, persecuted us, and perhaps said all manner of evil about us.

We need to give ourselves the gift of forgiveness. It is a gift that keeps on giving, because it liberates our souls, as well as our hearts and minds. We cannot receive all that God has for us and fulfill every aspect of our destiny if we hold bitterness and unforgiveness in our hearts.

When we simply cannot forgive another, no matter how hard we try, we must ask God to forgive that person through us. If we are sincere in our request, God will forgive the other person, not for us, but through us. We shall know that forgiveness has occurred when we are completely at ease in the presence of this person or at the mere mention of the person's name. I can't tell you how God accomplishes all of this. All I can say is that His ways are beyond finding out.

Everything Is On Time And In Order

"Why did this have to happen now?" Have you ever found yourself asking that question in response to some unexpected setback in your life? Or have you ever heard yourself saying, "This could not have happened at a worse time."

When we see life from God's perspective, we are given the wisdom to understand that *everything that happens in our life is on time and in order*. This has to be true if God is in absolute control of everyone and everything in the universe—and He is.

What causes so much unnecessary anguish, pain and suffering is our failure and refusal to see all circumstances squarely within the sovereign control of Almighty God.

God has lovingly instructed us in His Word that for the children of God, the followers of Christ, "(God causes) *all things (to) work together for good to them that love God, to them who are the called according to his purpose*" (Romans 8:28).

If we have made a commitment to walk each moment of each day in the path that God has carved out for us, then we shall not be shaken nor moved by the sudden, and sometimes catastrophic, events all around us. Neither shall we be moved by the evil tidings that cause paralyzing fear, trepidation and trembling in those who live by the world's view of circumstances.

The world's view of the "vicissitudes of life" renders one unable to see beyond the hand of man to the hand of God, orchestrating and controlling the most ostensibly insignificant detail of every worldly event and circumstance. And the late, great Bible teacher and lecturer, Oswald Chambers, tells us in *My Utmost for His Highest,* "Never believe that the so-called random events of life are anything less than God's appointed order. Be ready to discover His divine designs anywhere and everywhere."

God is above man and His hand controls the hand, as well as the heart, of man. Proverbs 21:1 informs us, "*The heart of the King is in the hand of the Lord; and He turns it as He turns the river.*" God's word also assures us that, "*...If God is for us, who can be against us?*" (Romans 8:31).

You might have to wait for years, as did Abraham and Sarah, for God to fulfill a promise made to you. Nevertheless, God's Word is true, and He will always come through. The Bible tells us, "*For Sarah conceived and bare Abraham a son in his old age, at the set time of which God had spoken to him*" (Genesis 21:2). If God did it for Abraham and Sarah, He'll do it for you. When doubts assail you, and discouragement seems to overtake you, your job is to trust and obey God, no matter how long He takes.

The Prophet Habakkuk counsels us, "*Slowly, steadily, surely the time approaches when the vision will be fulfilled. If it seems slow, do not despair, for these things will surely come to pass. Just be patient! They will not be overdue a single day!*" (Habakkuk 2:3, L.B).

"*What shall we then say to these things? If God be for us, who can be against us?*" (Romans 8:31).

God's order and time exceed man's intellectual comprehension. However, when we trust the heart of God, believe the Word of God, and surrender to the sovereignty of God, we know that *everything is on time and in order.*

You Are Blessed And Highly Favored

Right at this very moment, you are blessed and highly favored. No matter where you are situated in life, as a child of God, you are blessed and highly favored.

Your finances may be in disarray or may not be at all. Nevertheless, you are blessed and highly favored. You may be suffering with pain all over your body. Nevertheless, you are blessed and highly favored. You may have just experienced the home-going of the love of your life. Nevertheless, you are blessed and highly favored.

Your friends may be few and your enemies may be many. But you are blessed and highly favored. You may have been betrayed by your bosom buddy. But you are blessed and highly favored. You may have your good name smeared by the slanderer. But you are blessed and highly favored. You may have been lied about and hated. But you are blessed and highly favored.

You may have a problem that is so complicated that only God can unravel it. You are still blessed and highly favored. You may have been unjustly robbed of your earnings. You are still blessed and highly favored. Your social stock may have gone down, and the social invitations have dried up. You are still blessed and highly favored.

You may be in the midst of a fierce and violent battle for your life. However, you are blessed and highly favored. You may have asked, sought and knocked, all to no avail. However, you are blessed and highly favored.

No matter what the circumstance, situation or problem you may face, you are blessed and highly favored. *"You are blessed coming in and blessed going out. You are blessed in the city and blessed in the country. You are blessed eternally; with all the blessings Heaven has bestowed "*(Deuteronomy 28:3, 6).

"You Shall Reap What You Sow, More Than You Sow And Later Than You Sow"

During all of my childhood and for most of my adult life, I had repeated the premier principle of the farmer. It had also been a spiritual principle that I had heard my parents, grandmother and other close relatives advise: "You shall reap what you sow." It had proven to be an accurate description of what we can expect in terms of the fruit produced by our actions toward one another, whether at home or in the market place.

My grandmother's way of expressing what some have called *cosmic comeuppance* was: "Don't plant cabbage and expect collards to come up. Whatever you sow, that's exactly what you're going to reap. So you better be careful what you sow."

However, it was not until I was introduced to the ministry of Dr. Charles Stanley, Pastor of the First Baptist Church in Atlanta, that this spiritual truth was refined for me for the rest of my life. It was Dr. Stanley from whom I first heard it put as the title of this essay states: *"You shall reap what you sow, more than you sow and later than you sow."*

My grandmother owned an old Victorian house in the heart of Newark which still remains in our family. Every summer, she would buy packets of cabbage, collard and turnip greens seeds. She would plant them in the spring in her big back yard on Fairmount Avenue. The seeds were so tiny. I remember picking up a packet and shaking it around just to hear if anything was actually in the packet.

Once the seeds began to sprout above ground and then matured to full size, Mama would break off the leaves and gather them up to cook for dinner. I never told Mama how amazed I was at the entire process of sowing the tiny seeds and then reaping the big heads of cabbage and big leafed collard and turnip greens.

I just stared, and thought to myself, "No human being could accomplish this." I believe that this was one of my earliest childhood experiences that prompted me to begin to reverence the reality, power and presence of God. It certainly impacted the level of my faith. Call it my "collard greens theology."

The seed principle of sowing and reaping might be difficult to understand, but is certainly not difficult to practice. It works in every area of life: finance, relationships, good deeds, random acts of kindness, words of faith and encouragement, gift-giving, family support, prayer and meditation, praise and worship, unforgiveness, betrayal, covetousness, insecurity, fear and the full range of sinful acts.

Whether we have acknowledged it or not, we, in reality, are all farmers. Every day we sow seeds of every ilk and kind. If the crop coming up in your life is not what you want, perhaps you should check your seed bag. If the contents need changing, change them and don't delay. For if you do, cosmic comeuppance will pay a visit to you.

"You Catch More Flies With Honey Than You Do With Vinegar"

One of Mother's favorite sayings is "You catch more flies with honey than you do with vinegar." Mother's companion to this saying was "Be nice." As a child growing up, I must admit, that I cringed too many times to number at what I now regard as the centerpiece of Mother's homespun philosophy, reminiscent of Dale Carnegie's classic work, *How to Win Friends and Influence People.*

I have told Mother more than once in recent years that I have now lived long enough to verify that she was so right all along. When we are sweet and kind, warm and easy with people, they, in turn, become sweet and kind, warm and easy with us. It might take more than one encounter to make the difference, but don't give up. Then watch what happens.

People are virtually defenseless when being treated with sweetness and kindness. On the other hand, all their defenses go up when they are treated in a careless, insensitive, bitter-like fashion, or as Mother would describe it: "treated with vinegar." Most of us, when exposed to people with attitudes and dispositions drenched in vinegar, try escaping their presence. We say to ourselves, "There's no way they're going to catch this fly." Sometimes our escape is to get out of the person's life all together, through some form of alienation, separation, or termination of the relationship.

And yet, I've seen countless situations in which people just keep pouring vinegar on everything that touches and concerns them. And it's usually the people closest to them that are hit with splashes, if not the whole bottle, of vinegar. Others beyond their physical reach receive their dose of vinegar splashed either through the mail, a fax, a telephone call or an e-mail.

For years, I questioned what would cause a person to spray repeatedly what amounts to the vinegar of bitter words and behavior. But time spent in prayer and meditation on the Word of God, coupled with front-line experience in spiritual warfare, has served to subordinate my world-view perspective to the divine perspective.

Now when I come across fellow travelers trying to navigate the deep waters of life with a flask of vinegar in each hand, I can accurately predict that by the end of the day, they won't have one fly in their net. They have allowed the Enemy to trick them into believing that bitter words and behavior will cause people to draw nigh. However, the truth is that when we treat people with vinegar in our attitude, words and demeanor, they are not inclined to come near, but rather move away from us.

If we shall devote time reading and meditating on the Word of God, God will enable us to see ourselves from a godly perspective. Not only will our careless and insensitive treatment of others be revealed to us, but God will give us the courage, strength and discipline to turn from this evil bent in our life. With relative ease and comfort, we shall then be able to treat others with the love, care, respect and sensitivity that have been dipped in honey and is reflective of the image and likeness of Jesus.

Thank you, Mother.

"Look For The Dream That Keeps Coming Back. It Is Your Destiny."

What is it that you dream of being, doing, having, making, writing, creating, designing, producing, marketing, selling, building, managing, birthing? You dream this dream over and over again. It will not leave you alone. It will not. It cannot, because it is your destiny. Your dream keeps coming back because it needs you to live, and move, and manifest its destiny that is you.

Is there a dream that keeps coming back to you? A dream that won't let you go? A dream that you're afraid to share with even your best friend? A dream that comes to you by day and by night? A dream that wakes you up in the morning and puts you to sleep at night? A dream that you keep under a bushel for fear of being laughed at?

Is there a dream that always brings to mind Mama's constant admonition during my youth: *"You can do it if you don't doubt yourself."* A dream that resounds in Mother's biblical teaching: *"Always remember, if God has something for you, no demon in hell or earth can keep it from you."* A dream that causes the needed persistence of its accomplishment to be affirmed by Daddy's sterling philosophy that *"Dripping water will wear stone away."*

What is the dream that keeps coming back to you? What have you done with it? Have you "had a little talk with Jesus" about it? What is He saying? What has He told you to do about your dream that you haven't done yet? Have you taken the time to write out your goals? Have you followed the teaching of the prophet Habakkuk when he tells us:

> *"And the Lord answered me, and said, 'Write the vision, and make it plain upon tables, that he may run that readeth it.*
>
> *For the vision is yet for an appointed time, but at the end it shall speak, and not lie: though it tarry, wait for it; because it will surely come, it will not tarry.'"*
>
> Habakkuk 2:2, 3

What is holding you back from moving in the direction of your dream? Is it money? God has all the money that you'll ever need. Is it time? If you'll commit to becoming obsessed with the implementation of your dream, you'll take whatever time is necessary to make it happen. Remember, we all have the same amount of time — twenty-four flying hours, seven flying days a week. In this regard, our Father is the original "Equal Opportunity Employer."

Or perhaps you are well aware that it is a person in your life that is holding you back from the realization of your God-given dream. If this is your situation, your first order of business is to remove this person from your life — physically, emotionally and mentally — and in that order.

Prior to moving to Washington to work on Capitol Hill, I worked as a Senior Editor in the Broadcast Standards Department of NBC located at Rockefeller Plaza, in New York City. In the evening and after work, I attended a class in "Prosperity" taught by Dr. Eric Pace. One of Dr. Pace's instructions to us was that if you've removed someone from your physical life; don't allow them to remain in your mental life. However, as Christians, we must also release and let go of the relationship, in love, "with good to all concerned," by blessing the person, as they move away from us and toward the destiny of their dreams. This valuable teaching has proven to be a cherished treasure in my life.

It has been truthfully said that "If God gives the vision, He also gives the provision." And so the next time your dream comes back to you, kneel in prayer on the inside, get to work on the outside, and consider that dream that keeps coming back to you as already done in Jesus' Name. Amen.

"God Is Crazy About You"

Has anybody ever told you that God is crazy about you? Perhaps not. And the tragedy is that too often we have to become parents ourselves before we can begin to comprehend how crazy God is about us. I was reminded of this eternal truth some years ago when I was watching a television program, and overheard Marilyn Meberg, Christian author of *God At Your Wits' End*, make this astute remark about God's love for his children.

God's word to us says: *"The Lord has appeared of old unto me, saying, Yea, I have loved thee with an everlasting love; therefore with loving kindness have I drawn* thee" (Jeremiah 31:3). You might not agree, but I translate that to mean God is crazy about you and me. Further, He also assures us that *"You are precious to me, my little children."* That sounds like what I would say about my daughter, Regan Alexandria, and grandson, Jean-Pierre ("J.P.").

For most of us, God's love is simply incomprehensible. We want to understand and appreciate God's love for us, but our finite minds limit our understanding. Or the circumstances that confront and surround us are so overwhelming that we are unable to see God right in the middle of our circumstances.

A portrait painting of Jesus on the cross hangs on the wall in my bedroom. It was given to me by an American Peace Corps Volunteer during my husband's two year assignment in India as an Associate Peace Corps Director.

What has always been a haunting memory of the image of Jesus on the cross, even though my painting does not include them, are the falling tears that I always seem to see in my mind's eye. They are the tears of a broken heart of someone who is crazy about the one who has broken his heart.

Jesus died long before he was actually crucified on the cross. Jesus died of a broken heart in the Garden of Gethsemane. Jesus grieved himself to death in the Garden of Gethsemane. He grieved over the murdering hearts of His children that He was so crazy about.

Jesus is so crazy about each one of His children. He is willing to give us all the Father has and more. But we have become so duped by the lure of the world and its insatiable offerings that we are unable to return the Savior's unconditional love for us.

Then one day we find ourselves falsely accused. We find ourselves stealing away to our own Garden of Gethsemane. We find ourselves having to bear up under the weight of our own cross; having to endure the shunning, slights, insults, spit in our faces, humiliation, hurt, attacks, slander, and curses behind our back. We swoon and pass out at the first nail in our palm. We are not too proud to plead with the Father to let this cup pass. But, to our great disappointment, He won't even answer.

But then, thank God, I remember: He's still crazy about me. And if He's crazy about me, no matter the depth of my suffering, he's causing all these things to work together for my good, because I love God and I am called according to His divine purpose (Romans 8:28).

Thank you, God, for being so crazy about me that even my crucifying experience has been permitted by your eternal love for me. My crucifying experience has been divinely designed to fashion me into the image of your dear Son. It was your dear Son who scaled the depths of hell to bring me into a right relationship with the Father; who has proven, before the foundation of the world, that He is eternally crazy about me.

"Drink Deeply From Good Books, Especially the Bible"

Coach John Wooden, in his inspiring memoir entitled *Coach Wooden One-On-One*, (Regal Books: Ventura California, 2003) shares his dad's seven-point creed to live by. The fourth point of this creed was to *"Drink deeply from good books, especially the Bible."* Nothing compares to the knowledge and wisdom that lies between the covers of a good book.

Therefore, to live a godly, fruitful and soul-satisfying life, it is important that we drink, and drink deeply, from good books. Good books are defined as books that are written by authors who have been inspired by the Holy Spirit to pour forth words of wisdom and knowledge on the written page. Beginning with the Bible, which is the Word of God, we should establish our own library of written mentors, counselors, instructors, advisors, best friends, confidants and supporters.

Whether it is a difficult trial, a season of struggle in the valley, or the exhilaration of mountain top living, my Christian faith and consequent experience with the faithfulness of God have taught me that the Bible is the Word of God. And since it is the Word of God, it contains the first and last word on any earthly subject. The Bible contains all of the wisdom of the ages, from Genesis to Revelations.

To live is to experience life in all of its unseemly combinations, counterparts and pairs. Each experience has its mate and diametrically opposed opposite. Life is the mixture of the bitter and the sweet. If you are in the midst of experiencing one, rest assured the other is not far behind. Some of the pairs to which I refer are more than familiar to us. The experience of deep joy is designed to prepare us for deep sorrow. We would never know the meaning of sweet without having tasted the bitter.

Good books are of God. The author serves as a conduit for the Holy Spirit to channel its inspiration, wisdom, knowledge, instruction, and guidance to the reader. I consider and experience my good books as some of my best friends who sit on the shelf, waiting and ready to give me what wisdom and understanding I am in need of at the moment.

My good books eliminate my need to make a phone call, write a letter, send an e-mail or schedule a consultation appointment. They are right there, at my bedside, in my office, in the den, in the guest bedroom, in my bathroom. They remain poised, ready to be picked up, opened and drank from deeply.

If you haven't done so already, begin to gather around you the good books of your choice. The Holy Spirit will guide you in your selections. You will find that they will prove to be an investment that pays the highest of dividends that continue increasing. In fact, you will find that the stock of a good book goes only one way, and that is up.

My recommendation for the best gift you can give to a loved one, friend or colleague is a copy of a good book, especially the Bible. It never goes out of style. Its wisdom and knowledge increase in value and meaning, as you increase in the wisdom and knowledge of God.

It's Just A Holy Ghost Setup

No matter what you're going through, dear Friend, if you would, right now, begin to see it as nothing more than a Holy Ghost setup, you will discover that you have found the antidote to most of your pain and suffering.

You are God's child. He loves you unconditionally. In Matthew 7:11, Jesus tells us that *"If ye then, being evil, know how to give good gifts unto your children, how much more shall your Father which is in heaven give good gifts to them that ask him?"*

God knows exactly what kind of training and testing you need. God has not only determined what school you will attend, He has already mapped out your area of concentration while enrolled there. Your curricula are set and so are your teachers. All preparation has been designed to equip you to go out on the mission field of life. All resources have been provided to enable you to carry out your specific and unique assignment.

To see your circumstances as a mere Holy Ghost set-up for the divine manifestation in your life takes faith in God, a Man who does not—no, cannot lie. It also takes trust in the sovereignty of God over the circumstances of our life.

The late Dr. Charles Raymond Barker, Senior Pastor of the First Church of Religious Science in New York City used to say, *"It's not what to do, but what to know."* If we know that every detail of our life is circumscribed and controlled by God, we shall conduct our affairs in a characteristically calm and confident manner.

You must begin to see God as ordering and reordering, arranging and rearranging, ruling and overruling, all the events in your life. Admittedly, this takes tremendous faith. But it is our faith in the Word of God and the promises of God that moves the mighty hand of God on our behalf.

You must develop trust in God, as the child develops trust in his father and mother. The heavenly Father demands so little from His children. Even in the area of faith, God promises if we shall exercise faith the size of a grain of mustard seed, we shall witness magnificent and miraculous results.

Yes, dear Friend, every day and in every way, the Holy Ghost, in His infinite wisdom, is using every circumstance of our life, no matter how embarrassing or painful, as an opportunity to set us up for use in His Kingdom. We have been designed for a divine mission while here on earth. *Everything and everyone that touches our life, for good or ill, is a part of the Holy Ghost setup to position us exactly where God wants us to be.*

No matter how dire and disappointing things may seem today, if you will commit to trust the Lord and have patience in the outworking of His plan, you will experience victory in every area of your life. All you have to remember is to: *"Give, and it shall be given unto you; good measure, pressed down, and shaken together, and running over, shall men give into your bosom. For with the same measure that ye mete withal it shall be measured to you again"* (Luke 6:38).

"What Has God Told You To Do That You Haven't Done Yet?"

If we take the time to come apart and commune with the Lord, He will gently remind us of the one thing that He told us to do that we haven't done yet. Do you ever think of all the things you have asked God to do that He hasn't done yet? However, the more important question is: "What has God told you to do that you haven't done yet?"

If this describes your situation to a tee, perhaps your failure, and even refusal, to do what God has asked you to do is the only accurate explanation for your long list of unanswered prayers. God not only knows our prayers before we pray them; He has also answered our prayers before we pray them. This is why doing what God has told you to do is so important.

Our prompt obedience to God's instruction is inextricably tied to the time, manner and magnitude of God's answer to our prayers. In the Gospel of Luke, the fifth chapter, it is reported that one day Jesus was standing on the shore of Lake Gennesaret.

The crowd was pressing in on Jesus to hear the teaching of the Word of God. Jesus noticed that two boats had been left by the fishermen, while they were out scrubbing their nets. Jesus climbed into Simon's boat and began using it as a pulpit to teach the crowds.

The following exchange between Jesus and Simon reveal the precious fruits of prompt, unqualified and courageous obedience to the Master:

> *"When he finished teaching, he said to Simon, 'Push out into deep water and let your nets out for a catch.'*
> *Simon said, 'Master, we've been fishing hard all night and haven't caught even a minnow. But if you say so, I'll let out the nets.'*
> *It was no sooner said than done—a huge haul of fish, straining the nets past capacity.*

> *They waved to their partners in the other boat to come help them. They filled both boats, nearly swamping them with the catch."*
>
> Luke 5:4-7 (MSG)

God instructs us to *launch out into the deep* and accomplish a particular goal, realize our fondest dream, fulfill an obligation, renew our minds in some particular area, or begin to adopt a godly perspective about everything.

For example, He tells us to start a business, join a church, take a course, forgive another, write a book, run for office, return a favor, attend a retreat, terminate a relationship, or change our career. Sometimes He simply says, "Go to work!" But we are not willing to go deep. We remain on the shore. We later discover that "our shore-line living has produced God's shoreline giving." We also learn that shoreline living teaches us that "God can only do for us what He can do through us."

We hear Him with the physical outer ear, but we remain hard of hearing with the spiritual inner ear. At first, He speaks quietly. Later, He speaks loudly. However, we still put off and procrastinate. We hesitate. We take what God has told us to do and put it on the back burner.

Our prayer requests remain on the front burner. We become so busy with our prayer requests (and why God hasn't answered them) that we wind up taking God off the stove completely. After all, more room on the stove is needed for our mounting prayer requests. Our impatience and arrogance keep us in a "Why hasn't God answered?" mode.

In the meantime, God patiently waits. He waits for those of us who will *dare to believe, defy the odds and dare to obey.* When we obey God, no matter how foolish it may seem to others, God begins to answer our prayers. We must trust the faithfulness of God, even when we can't trace the hand of God.

In the midst of our prompt and diligent obedience to do what God has told us to do that we haven't done yet, we suddenly realize that in His will is our peace. In His will are the answers to all our prayers. In His will is so much more than we could have ever asked or imagined.

"Give Other People What They Don't Deserve When They Need It The Most"

Sometime ago, while listening to the radio, I heard Pastor Chip Ingram, host of the radio broadcast, "Living On the Edge," exhort his church congregation, and those in the listening radio audience, to *"Give other people what they don't deserve when they need it the most."* This can be considered to be the clarion call of the universe to all Christians. It follows right on the heels of the Golden Rule. The Golden Rule states that, in our interactions with others, we "Do unto others as we would have them do unto us."

Periodically, we all need someone in our life that cares enough to give us what we don't deserve when we need it the most. Many of us would call such a person an angel of mercy. I call such an individual none other than Jesus operating through His beloved saints in the world who allow Him to use them as channels of blessings.

Is this not what our Father did for us at the Cross? Did He not sacrifice the shed blood of His only Son in payment for the redemption of the sins of mankind? And is this not what Jesus does for us every minute of every hour? Does He not give us what we don't deserve when we need it the most?

The way to insure that God will always send you someone to give you what you don't deserve when you need it the most is to be available for God to use you to be His angel of mercy for someone else.

No human satisfaction compares to the satisfaction that comes from allowing God to use us as vessels and channels of blessing for another. The reason for this is that we have the character of Christ deeply embedded in our spirits, souls and sinew. It's there whether we want to acknowledge it or not.

And the chief character of Christ is the unconditional love with which He loves us. It is the agape love that Martin Luther King, Jr. often referred to.

If you want to be greatly blessed and highly favored, begin to give others that cross your path, whether friend or foe, what they don't deserve and when they need it the most.

Become an Ambassador for Christ in your giving and forgiving. If you do, there will be rivers of blessing, the tides of which will be so high and wide, you will not have room to receive it all. They shall come in like a flood and overtake you.

A Lifestyle of Humility

Nothing pleases the Father more than our pursuit and practice of a lifestyle of humility. Nothing assures the answers to our prayers and the action of God on our behalf, even when we fail to pray, as does a spirit of humility. When we are genuinely humble, we are not proud or haughty, arrogant or assertive. We, moment-by-moment, defer and submit, in our attitudes and actions, to the Holy Spirit that resides within our bodies, the temples of the Holy Ghost.

We exhibit the spirit of humility when we are unpretentious in all our ways. We are simply who God made us to be. We don't spend precious time trying to be who we are not and who God never intended us to be. Humility was the centerpiece of the life of Christ. Therefore, above all the Christian attributes, it is the chief characteristic of the follower of Christ. Jesus humbled himself by surrendering to the Father's will, even unto death.

In 1 Peter 5:6-7, we are told to *"Humble yourselves under the mighty hand of God, that He may exalt you at the proper time, casting all your anxiety upon Him, because He cares for you."* And in another passage of Scripture, 2 Chronicles 7:13-14, we are promised that "*...if we humble ourselves, pray, seek God's face, and repent, then God will hear from heaven and heal our land."*

The spirit of humility in the child of God is exercised when we stop to ask at every juncture or fork in the road, "Father, what would you have me do, not do, say, not say, give, not give, see, not see, be or not be in this situation?" This check-in with the Father expresses our willingness to submit to His plans, His ways and His time in whatever matters we are facing. Would we not agree that God deserves no less in terms of the reverence, respect and submission that comprise the component parts of humility?

Our attitude of humility allows God to do for us what we acknowledge that we cannot do for ourselves. We acknowledge that without Him, we cannot take our next breath; open our eyes; see with eyes that are open; think our next thought; swallow our next mouthful of food; stand up, sit up; lie down; walk without stumbling or falling; hear a bird sing, taste the bitter and sweet, and know the difference; smell the fresh air of morning; feel the joy of a hug; talk, sing, dance, skip, march, run or clap our hands in praise. In humility, we acknowledge that we can do nothing without Him. Nothing. Not any thing at all.

Humble believers recognize Jesus as Lord over all. We also realize that if we are to get ahead in life then we must put and keep Jesus as the head of our life in every detail and particular. We must resolve that in our getting ahead, we must not get ahead of the Holy Spirit. We must keep Him in front, in charge and in command, no matter what the cost—and the cost can be expensive from the world's point of view.

No matter what you may be facing at this time, resist the temptation to become anxious and worried. Resist the temptation to manipulate circumstances to your liking. Trust the love, mercy and grace of the Lord Jesus Christ to know what is best for you. Surrender to His holy plan and purpose for your life, and all that you hold dear. Your humility before the Lord will then usher you into the throne room of the Almighty to be exalted at the proper time, in His own way and in His own time.

"Withdraw From Those Who Continually Find Fault With You"

Many times our success in fulfilling our God-given assignment is being hampered by those in our midst who continually find fault with us. It could be a parent, a spouse, a friend, an employer, a teacher, a co-worker, or our next door neighbor. In other words, the people who find fault with us are often those closest to us, and not within the circle of obvious or officially declared adversaries.

In his *Seeds of Wisdom on Motivating Yourself* (The Wisdom Center: Denton, Texas, 2003, pp. 23-26), Dr. Mike Murdock advises that unhealthy relationships drain us mentally and emotionally. He further counsels that if you are to maintain energy that is a necessary ingredient in any success, you must "...Withdraw from those who stay unhappy with you...without a true reason and cause. Withdraw from those who continually find fault with you...though you are emptying your very life out daily. Withdraw from those who feel insulted when you do not telephone them...though your own life seems overwhelming and you cannot get everything done."

Our Heavenly Father has made us perfectly for our divine purpose on the earth. However, our perfection is developmental and not staid and static. Therefore, as we journey through life, we inevitably encounter and interact with those who are less attuned to that within us that is uniquely made in the image and likeness of God. The world is more attuned to that within us that still struggles to become all that we are in God's sight.

Those who specialize in faultfinding are usually those who refuse to look at their own faults, and spend time working on their own issues. The Bible tells us before we take the mote out of our brother's eye; we must first remove the beam in our own eye. Matthew 7:5.

As children of the Most High God, we must consider it a plus when our nerves are sometimes plucked by those who would find fault with us. If such negative attention causes us to draw closer to God, God has used the faultfinder to bless us. Once again, the biblical promise of Romans 8:28, "*(God causes) all things to work together for good to them that love God, to them who are the called according to his purpose,"* has preempted any evil plan that might be afoot.

Our withdrawal may not be physical. Our circumstances are often such that it cannot be. There are times when the Father has intentionally designed our withdrawals to be spiritual. That means that we guard our hearts from those who make it their business to find fault with us. We keep secret, and therefore, sacred, our hopes, dreams and the desires of our hearts. We talk to Jesus about the longings of our heart; what we'd like to be, to do and to achieve in life. We don't make the colossal mistake of Joseph. That is, we don't share the dreams that God has given us to those whose envy and jealousy will cause them to conspire against us. However, if it is a part of God's plan that we make such a mistake, we know that God shall always turn it for His glory and our good.

When we are under attack by the faultfinders, we must run to the throne of grace at every hour, of every day, if need be. We stay in the Word of God, meditating on the promises, being reminded that we serve an all-knowing, all-powerful, all-wise and ever-present God. We allow God's Word to remind us that He is sovereign; that He makes no mistakes; and as author Marilyn Meberg has squarely put it: *He is militantly in control.* (see *God At Your Wits' End*).

Yes, it is our Father who allows the faultfinders in our lives. And it is also our Father who sits on the throne of grace waiting for us to come and talk to Him about it.

On this point, I'm reminded of the following lyrics of an old gospel song, "Just A Little Talk," that we sang in Sunday school and church when I was a child: "Now let us have a little talk with Jesus...Let us tell Him all about our troubles...You will find a little talk with Jesus makes it right, makes it right."

"This Is the Life God Has Called Me To"

When you are experiencing brokenness in your life in the form of hardship, difficulty and pain, you must yield to God's Holy Will and confess, "This is the life God has called me to." If your bills are stacked so high that you can't see over them, you must yield and confess, "This is the life God has called me to."

If your children disobey you and your in-laws berate you, you must yield and confess, "This is the life God has called me to." If you're out of work and out of prospects, you must yield and confess, "This is the life God has called me to."

When your lot is the fiery furnace or the deep waters, you must yield and confess, "This is the life God has called me to." If your mate has been unfaithful and your best friend has betrayed you, you must yield and confess, "This is the life God has called me to." When you are experiencing deep disappointment or never ending heartache, you must yield and confess, "This is the life God has called me to." When there's sickness in your body and you can't seem to get well, you must yield and confess, "This is the life God has called me to."

Our confession and surrender is not an act of resignation, but an affirmation of recognition and reliance on the providence of a Mighty God Who is able to do exceedingly, abundantly above all that we could ever ask, think or imagine.

L.B. Cowman, speaking poignantly, if not poetically, of the purpose and meaning of brokenness in our lives, informs us that "God never uses anyone to a great degree until He breaks the person completely. Joseph experienced more sorrow than the other sons of Jacob and it led him into a ministry of food for all the nations. For this reason the Holy Spirit said of him, '*Joseph is a fruitful vine... near a spring whose branches climb over a wall.*' Genesis 49:22. It takes sorrow to expand and deepen the soul."

It is our confession and surrender to God's sovereign plan and purpose for our life that ushers us into the presence of the Lord. In His presence we are imbued with His power, His protection, His provision and His peace. We are then enabled to do the *"greater works"* that have been ordained by the Father as our God-given mission in the earth. *"Verily, verily, I say unto you, He that believeth on me, the works that I do shall he do also; and greater works than these shall he do; because I go unto my Father"* (John 14:12).

The Holiness of Closed Doors

Just before my relocation to Washington following the Presidential Inauguration of Jimmy Carter, I had been selected as one of three final candidates for an attorney position with two different major pharmaceutical corporations in New York City. I was naturally excited about the prospect of entering corporate America at this level. Given my litigation experience at the New York City Corporation Counsel; and solid legal training at Rutgers University Law School, I considered myself more than equipped to use and further develop my skills as an attorney in a corporate environment.

Nevertheless, shortly thereafter, I was hit with a double whammy when I was notified by both companies, back-to-back, that I had not been selected as the final candidate. My spirits sagged and old, but very familiar, disappointment nagged at my heart and soul. I would refuse to despair. Instead, I would do as David did when faced with some form of disappointment, I would encourage myself by standing on the Word of God. Moreover, I would remind myself that my disappointment was His appointment.

If I believed that God was controlling the situation, I would quietly rejoice and give praise and glory to the Father. Intuitively, I knew that these doors would not open again. I also knew that while both doors to these new professional opportunities had been physically closed by man; the closing had been spiritually engineered and orchestrated by God. In accordance with His divine plan and purpose for my life, and the lives of others that would be touched and blessed by my work, God knew that these doors had to close.

Several weeks later, and still mildly grieving the loss of these closed doors, I received a telephone call from my brother Rob (Robert B. Washington, Jr.). A prominent attorney in Washington, Rob was also Chairman of the local Democratic Party. He had called to invite me and other family members to the Inaugural Ball and related inaugural activities. At some point during our brief conversation, I casually remarked that while I respected the fact that he would be busy during the week of the inaugural festivities, nevertheless, perhaps we could talk about my interest in job opportunities in Washington.

Thereafter, Rob arranged for me to meet with the late Congressman Stewart B. McKinney (R-CT) the morning after the Inaugural Ball. "Stew," as he insisted on being called by everyone, offered me the job of Minority (Republican) Chief Counsel and Staff Director of the House Committee on the District of Columbia. I joyously accepted and was hired on the spot.

The offer of the Congressional appointment, right on the heels of the loss of two back-to-back professional opportunities, served to dramatically teach me for all time the spiritual principle of the Holiness of Closed Doors. If I had been selected by either pharmaceutical company as the candidate of their choice, I would not have broached the subject with my brother about job opportunities in Washington. Rather, I would have been busily mastering the nuts and bolts of my new position. In fact, I might not even have attended the Inaugural Ball at all, given my innate dedication to my work.

And so it was God's divine plan and purpose for my life that kept the doors to the pharmaceutical companies closed. God knew that He had a much bigger and better door that He was about to open widely for me. He also knew that this experience would teach me, in a mighty and magnificent way, the spiritual lesson that, based on God's unconditional love for me, my disappointment would always be just a prelude to His divine appointment.

Sometimes the blessings God has for us have our names on them. However, they are sequestered behind closed doors. In God's time, He shall open the door. We must wait, no matter how long it takes.

Paul and his companions were restrained by the Holy Spirit from preaching the Word in the province of Asia. Specifically, the Scripture says, "*Now when they had gone throughout Phrygia and the region of Galatia, and were forbidden of the Holy Ghost to preach the word in Asia...*" (Acts 16:6).

If what is behind the closed door is designed and reserved for us, a light tap on the door will cause the door to swing wide open. Sometimes if what is behind the closed door is for us, our mere appearance before the door will cause the door to swing wide open.

Usually these are confirmations of the fact that God's providential hand is on the proverbial door knob.

When we feel so strongly that we must have what is behind the door, but the door remains shut, we need to stop, stay obedient, trust God and wait. When we feel tempted to crash a door or kick in a door, we can be assured that this is not of God. He has promised that our battle with closed doors is not ours, but His. Therefore, we must let the Lord fight it on our behalf. Our only fight is the fight of faith; faith in the promises of God to do all that He has promised.

And so the next time you are faced with a closed door, the first thing you must do is thank God for the closed door. The second thing you must do is commit the closed door into the keeping of the Almighty to open the door or keep it closed according to His divine will and purpose for your life. The third and final thing you must do is recognize that often a closed door is God's sign to you that He is about to open a bigger and better door for you, the one that is consistent with you divine destiny.

You will never regret that you did.

Discipline

Nothing takes the place of discipline in one's life. Talent won't. Good looks won't. Money won't. The right social and political connections won't. College degrees won't. Even prayer, without discipline, is devoid of its power. Discipline is simply self-control placed under the umbrella of God's control. It usually involves some aspect of self-denial in certain areas of our life.

God has endowed each individual with unique skills and talents. But without discipline, our talents wither and die. Talent is typically touted as the *sine qua non* of success. But talent is often overrated. Consequently, I am inclined to agree with Martin Ritt when he stated: *"I don't have a lot of respect for talent. Talent is genetic. It's what you do with it that counts."*

For the student, discipline is doing your homework every day, and without fail. For the Christ-like Christian, it is walking the walk and not just talking the talk; it is carrying your cross with grace and humility; and against all odds when necessary; it is staying in touch with your Guide on the inside; it is devoting quality time each day to prayer and meditation. For the artist and the athlete alike, discipline may be summed up in three words: practice, practice, practice.

For the person who wants to lose weight, it is the time given to the humble consideration—not so much to what you're eating—but what's eating you. For the individual who longs to attract the right mate into his or her life, it's the precious time given to being the right person, and then patiently allowing God, in His own way and in His own time, to usher the right person into your life.

No matter how artistically, intellectually, or physically endowed we may be, without discipline, we will never come into the fullest use of our divine potential. In the astute words of author Sandra Felton on this point, "The world is waiting to be ennobled by our fullest participation." Without discipline, we are hamstrung from fully participating in life by doing the one thing that only we can do. Discipline, in any field of endeavor, is doing, with commitment and resolve daily, that one thing that is prerequisite to the ultimate achievement of a specific goal.

Discipline stands up to delay, disappointment and discouragement. It does not throw in the towel at the first sign of defeat or delay in any arena. Discipline says, "I can" when everyone around you is saying "You can't." Discipline is careful not to see delay as denial, but as an intentional part of God's plan and, therefore, sacred.

Discipline is the mother hen that sows the seed, waters the ground, fertilizes the soil, harvests the wheat, grinds the wheat and finally bakes the bread that was her desired goal from the very beginning of her dream process and imagination, under girded by discipline.

You Are Different, But Not Defective

We are all different. We might be born with the same ethnic and cultural background, in the same country, or even in the same family. Nevertheless, we are all different. We are different by God's design; different, but not defective. To fail to acknowledge that we are different is to dishonor God. To question why we are different is to second-guess God.

Each of us is made in the image and likeness of God. We come into the world inherently full of His grace and power. God has brought us to the world at the right time, through the right parents, and in the right order. Moreover, "He has created us for such a time as this."

As children of God, we must be committed to recognizing that our differences have been designed by God as a part of His intentional plan and purpose. Our distinct differences enable us to fulfill our special and unique assignment in the world.

So many of our children are growing up in homes where, verbally or through mistreatment and abuse, they are being told by their parents or guardians that they are defective because they are different. However, just the opposite is true. It is the godly cultivation of your difference that will distinguish you in the world. Moreover, the Bible tells us that "*A man's gift maketh room for him, and bringeth him before great men*" (Proverbs 18:16). Nevertheless, many of our children attend schools every day in which the overriding message that is communicated to them—however non-verbally or inadvertently— is that because they are different, they are defective.

The Holy Scriptures also tell us that "*God has made us and not we ourselves.*" God doesn't make junk, and He doesn't make any mistakes. God has made you and every aspect of your physical being and personality, according to His divine plan and purpose for your life. God created you and then discarded the mold from which you were made. You are the only "you" that exists in the universe. There is none like you; no, not one.

You are made in God's image and likeness. You don't have to allow others to cause you to fear your differences. Remember, "*For*

God hath not given us the spirit of fear, but of power and of love and of a sound mind" (2 Timothy 1:7). You will know that you have reached a certain level of spiritual maturity when you are able to love yourself, with all of your differences, and to realize that your differences are divinely designed to enable you to carry out the special work that God has carved out for you in the world.

Call Back

When we find ourselves the target of severe and unrelenting satanic attack, there is no balm sweeter than that of a *call back* from a fellow traveler. A *call back* is the testimony that we share with one another of how God brought us through our own personal brand of persecution, hardship and trial. No prescription or over-the-counter medicine can compare with the testimony of one who has been the recipient of God's presence, power, protection, provision and peace. A "call back" nourishes our souls and strengthens our resolve to stay on the straight and narrow path until the Father calls us home. We don't feel as afraid or as insecure.

On this journey through life, some of us are further up the road, in our experience of tests, hardships and trying times. We have, with God's grace, even endured those times when we seemed to have served as Satan's kick ball of choice. Satan would have us look in our mirror and agree that we have been beaten to a pulp. He has almost convinced us that we are down for the count. But something would not let us give up, give in or give out. This "something" was nothing but the providence of God that brought us through to glorious victory and success in Jesus Christ.

God uses these times of tests and trials to teach us valuable lessons. In addition to gaining a more intimate knowledge of the power and presence of God, we learn, as did Joseph, that *what others meant for evil, God meant it for our good* (Genesis 50:20). A knowledge of this lesson gives cause for praise and rejoicing the next time we find ourselves in a pit experience, clad in prison garb, but nevertheless on our way to the palace.

But God doesn't want us to stop there. It is not enough for us to experience the saving grace of God in the midst of persecution and trial. It is our divine duty to call back and tell other believers that our God will see them through; that our God is a wonder-working God; that He is El Shaddai, the God who is more than enough. As El Shaddai, He has promised that if He doesn't have what we need, He will make it for us!

We have an eternal obligation to call back and tell how God was with us in our fiery furnace; and when we escaped, not one strand of our hair was singed; to call back and tell how God rescued us from financial disaster, strain and stress. As followers of Christ, we have a duty to call back and tell how God brought the right mate into our lives; to call back and tell how God healed our body, when the doctors threw in the towel after their medicines would do no good.

It is our duty to call back and tell how God opened the right door for employment when everything looked bleak; to call back and tell how God served as our lawyer in the courtroom. Jesus expects us to call back and tell how God was with us in the deep waters and the waters did not drown us; to call back and tell how we prayed, turned our back to the lions, and God shut the lions' mouths.

Jesus called back.

Paul and Daniel called back. Shadrack, Meshack and Abednego called back. Abraham and Sarah called back. Mother Mary and Mary Magdalene called back. Job and Joseph called back. Hannah and Abigail called back. Queen Esther called back. David and Jehoshophat called back. Ruth and Naomi called back.

Mama called back. Mother and Daddy called back. Hardy called back. Our aunts, uncles, and cousins called back. Our elders, government and community leaders called back. Our public school teachers and administrators called back. Our church saints, officers and clergy called back. Our Sunday school teachers and mentors called back. Our camp counselors and "neighborhood house" directors and staff members called back.

The "call back" legacy is the greatest legacy that any parent or grandparent, people or nation can leave to future generations. It is the legacy of the blessed assurance of God's faithfulness to His children.

No Evil Design Can Trump the Plan and Purpose of God

One of the perennial mysteries of the Bible is that God's providence is at work in the most horrific circumstances of human evil. Because God is sovereign in the universe, He is over all and controls all. God, by His very nature, is omnipotent, omniscient and omnipresent. Therefore, it can be reasonably assumed that it took a spirit-filled believer to wisely and rightly observe that, "No human evil can trump the providence of God."

Where evil exists or even flourishes, it does so by the permissive will of God. Evil, in any form or degree, cannot exist outside of the ultimate plan and purpose of the Almighty God. That is why we don't have to worry, fret or fear when evil draws near. We must rely, in faith, upon our Father to help us, protect us, provide for us and shepherd us through troubled times. In Psalm 46, David reminds us that "God *is our refuge and strength, a very present help in trouble.*"

No matter how much Satan appears to have the upper hand or the winning hand, He, along with everything else and everybody else, is controlled by the Most High God. Moreover, Satan has been described by the Word of God as *a defeated foe.* He has already lost. We have already won. As ministers of the Gospel enjoy admonishing us: "Read the back of the Book! We win!"

In reality, we don't have to read the back of the Bible to know that we win. All we have to do is allow Jesus to take our hand and lead us by His Holy Spirit along the path of life carved out for us by the Father. Psalm 138:7 tells us: "*Though I walk in the midst of trouble, thou wilt revive me; thou shalt stretch forth thine hand against the wrath of mine enemies and thy right hand shall save me.*"

Evil is expert at parading around pretending that it is in charge and all powerful. But evil can only exist in the confines of Romans 8:28. In this eternal Scripture, spoken by Paul to the Romans, God assures us that He, and He alone "... *(causes) all things to work together for good to them that love God, to them who are the called according to his purpose.*"

In Romans 8:37, Paul again exhorts us: *"In all these things, we are more than conquerors through him who loved us."* Therefore, we have the promise of the Father that no evil design, however wicked or comprehensive, can trump the plan and purpose of God.

She Takes No Tea For The Fever

My Father's mother, whom we all called Mama, because Daddy called her Mama, was always teaching lessons to me and all those with whom she came in contact. Usually Mama's lessons could be summed up in one of her pet expressions, indelibly impressed upon my conscious, subconscious and any other conscious mind known and unknown to me. One such life lesson was summed up in Mama's pet expression, "Take no tea for the fever."

Mama revered the memory of her Father, Ben Bradley, known by us as Grandpa. She would often tell me in talking about him, how in Blakely, Georgia, where she grew up, there wasn't anybody in town that Grandpa wouldn't stand up to. Mama was born in 1899, so this was back in the early 1900's when she was a child. During those days, Grandpa could have lost his life in an instance by standing up to certain members of this small, southern community. Nevertheless, Grandpa characteristically stood tall, faced his opponents of the hour, and "took no tea for the fever," no matter what the nature of the situation was.

Mama said "when" confronted by difficult problems and situations manifesting as fever in the body; stand up and face the situation head on. Mama stressed the "when" and not "if confronted;" because as sure as you're born, you're going to be confronted with difficult circumstances and stressful situations for as long as you live. Nevertheless, Mama said, "Do what you can. Do what's in your power to solve the problem." In other words, do what you can to get rid of the fever; just don't take tea for the fever. Because taking tea for the fever is not an antidote for the fever. Taking tea merely allows you to do something that perhaps gives you temporary or even momentary relief. But the root cause of the fever is still there; and your temperature is still rising.

Continuing with Mama's metaphor, a fever tells us that there's disease in the body. It's the body's way of alerting us that something is very wrong; and that an appropriate remedy needs to be applied and applied quickly. There is no time for taking tea. To take tea under these circumstances is to ignore the root cause of the problem.

Ignoring the root cause of the problem only leads to a bigger, more serious problem.

A fever in the body is like the red light that goes off in the car that tells us that our seat belt is not on, or that we're down to four gallons of gas. How foolish it would be to keep driving, ignoring the red light until we're either out of gas altogether, or run the risk of being ejected from our vehicle in the case of an accident.

Mama in no way was disparaging the taking of tea. In fact, Mama drank as much tea as anyone I ever knew. But when faced with a big problem in her life, Mama's way was to put the teacup in the saucer, put the teapot on the back burner of the stove, and address her problem head-on. Mama didn't waste valuable time ducking and dodging the problem, hoping it would go away, or worst yet, pretending it wasn't there at all. Neither should we waste valuable time ducking and dodging the problem and pretending it's not there.

Mama's philosophy, if not contention, was that prayer was the mightiest weapon that you can use in the solution to any problem. She said she never had a problem that God couldn't solve. After you've asked God to help you solve your problem, Mama said you'll notice little ideas coming to you that you never had before. In answer to our prayer, God will usually instruct us to take certain action; to move your feet. It may or may not involve other people. For instance, He might tell you to spend more quality time in His Word; go back to church; find a good Christian attorney; see a medical specialist; or seek a good Christian counselor. Often, God will simply tell you to be still and to listen for His still, small voice.

While you're listening for God to answer you with the solution to your problem, it is important to know that God has already solved the problem. He is just waiting to get your attention to show you how to appropriate it in your life. How about that! The God of the universe, kept waiting by us to show us, give us, bless us with what we need. However, we have been known to take years to give Him our attention. How many times have we made a request of someone, and then gone on with the busyness of our lives. By the time we finally get back to the person, the person matter-of-factly tells us that they have what we requested but they were waiting for us to get back to them. Or that they tried to reach us on several occasions but our line was busy, and consequently they couldn't get through.

Mama had it right. God is displeased when we take tea for the presenting fever of a giant problem in our life. Our Almighty God wants us to stand up, turn around and face our problems head on. Paul tells us in 2 Timothy 1:7, *"For God hath not given us the spirit of fear; but of power, and of love, and of a sound mind."* This means that we have everything that we need to solve our problems, no matter what form they may take.

So the next time you're faced with what may seem to be the fever of an insurmountable problem, the first thing you must do is put that tea cup down. Then, in meditation day and night on the Word of God, begin to appropriate the power, love and sound mind of the Holy Spirit that you have been given by the Father to use in a mighty and magnificent way to solve every imaginable problem that you face.

Thank you, Mama.

Take the Loss and Move On

Sometimes it becomes necessary to take a loss and move on. Our human inclination wants to demand our rights, stay and fight; seek a second opinion, hire an investigator, retain a lawyer, or go around the mountain just one more time. But then there is the quiet voice of the Holy Spirit that whispers, *"Let it go. Bow out. Walk away. Hands off. Give it to me. Let Me handle it for you."*

When we are faced with loss—loss of a job, loss of a loved one, loss of our health, loss of our money, or loss of a relationship, we are being challenged by our indwelling Lord to know that there is no loss in Spirit. There is no loss in Christ Jesus. When we are faced with loss of any kind, we are merely being transitioned to our next right place on the path of our spiritual journey— a journey that has been divinely designed by God.

No matter how anguished you may be at the time, know that God still holds you in the palm of His hand, and that you are safe for all eternity. He has promised never to leave you alone. At the Last Supper, Jesus told His Disciples that He was going away, but that He was sending them another Comforter, the Holy Spirit, who would be with them until the end of time. John 14:16; 15:26; 16:7. As heirs of God and joint heirs with Christ, He is our Comforter, too.

In Romans 8:28, we are reminded: *"And we know that all things work together for good to them that love God, to them who are the called according to his purpose."* Since God is a man that does not lie, our loss must be gain if we properly place it in the context of our Christian faith, and see it from God's perspective. We can't lose with the promises of God set forth in His Word.

When you are faced with circumstances that spell deep anguish and loss, stop and affirm the words of Joseph to his brothers: *"What you intended for evil, God intended for good"* (Genesis 50:20). Then go forward in an attitude of praise, glory and honor to the Father that He loved you so much that He planned to be involved in every detail of your life, turning ashes into beauty; loss into gain; pain into power; disappointment into His appointment.

We have but one overriding responsibility in the face of loss, and that is to surrender all to Jesus. Our loss is just as much a part of the Father's plan and purpose for our life as is what the world calls gain.

If we are faithful to trust in the Father's unconditional love, and His willingness to give us only what is best for our life, then when loss rings the bell at the front door or leaves its package at the back door, we can answer with our head held high and unbowed, although perhaps bruised and bloodied. We can answer with a submitted will and resolve that is aligned with God's plan and purpose.

Claim Your Right to Say "No."

You will never be able to use your gifts and talents to the maximum, in service to God, or to fulfill your divine mission in the earth, if, in the use of your time and talents, you continually fail to claim your right to say, "No." From the Master's perspective, the use of your time and talents is nothing less than sacred. Our time and talents are not only sacred, but precious. The use of our time and talents is for the exclusive purpose of the fulfillment of our earthly mission, as ordained by God's divine plan.

No matter by whom, what, where and why demands are being made upon you, you have the God-given right to say "No." In fact, it is your bounden duty to say, "No," if you are to fulfill your mission, planned for you by Almighty God before the foundation of the world. No dialogue is more fitting in the context of the importance of your need to say "No" to the numerous demands made on you by others; demands essentially extraneous to your divine assignment, than the contemporary query: "What is it about 'No' that you don't understand?"

Often, when we are presented with various proposals from friends, family and others, in the use of our time, we hesitate, before finally saying "No." Or, worse yet, we say "Yes" with our lips, but our mind and heart silently scream "No." In these situations, our "Yes" is designed to please others, even at the cost of displeasing our Father. Who comes first in your life? Is it your family and friends or your heavenly Father? Doesn't the Bible tell us that *"When my father and my mother forsake me, then the Lord will take me up"* (Psalm 27:10). It doesn't say "if." It says "when." That means there will be times in our life when we shall be disappointed or feel abandoned, even by our Mother and Father.

When people are pulling on us to do this or that, go here or there, join this or that; it behooves us to respond to others as Jesus responded to His family members when they demanded use of His time, attention and talents. Jesus said, *"I must be about my Father's business"* (Luke 2:49). Those are words we all need to meditate on day and night. As followers of Christ, we are here to be about God's business for as long as we're here on earth. If we will take time and listen, the Holy Spirit is continually advocating the right ordering, from God's perspective, of our priorities.

The Bible tells us to "Seek *ye first the Kingdom of God, and all these things shall be added unto us*" (Matthew 6:33). In other words, if we take care of God's business, God shall take care of our business. If we shall pursue, with all our might, His vision for our life, He shall provide whatever we need spiritually and materially. Spiritually, He shall provide us with His peace, strength, joy, faith, comfort, trust, security and favor. Materially, He shall provide us with the right food, clothes, shelter, and employment. He shall also provide us with needed transportation, godly friendships and companionship.

Saying "No" in love, and from the godly perspective of your role in the world, will, in fact, draw others to you as they are blessed by the fruit produced by the anointed performance of your God-given assignment. It takes courage to say "No" to the world's alluring demands on the use of our time and talents. It also takes courage to answer the call of Him who loves us unconditionally, and is more than enough to meet and even exceed the need of the hour. It takes faith to believe in a heavenly Father who "... *is able to keep you from falling, and present you faultless before the presence of his glory with exceeding joy...the only wise God, our Savior, be glory and majesty, dominion and power, both now and ever. Amen*" (Jude 1: 24-25).

Let Your Appearance Commend Christ

The question that is probably asked in our society more than any other, and on a daily basis, is "What shall I wear?" or "What shall I put on?" And then there are the follow-up questions of "Is it okay?" "Is it in?" "Is it out?"

From one generation to the next, there are always words-on-top-of-words regarding one's appearance. The follow-up questions are endless: "Is my outfit in? Will I look ridiculous? Please tell me the truth." We prance around in style in shoes that punish the divine design of our feet. We strut around, breathless, in clothes that pinch and chafe.

The Bible tells us that we are Ambassadors for Christ. Simply put, we do not represent ourselves in the world; we represent Jesus. Therefore, our appearance should, in all ways and at all times, commend Christ. Our hairstyle should commend Him. Our make-up should commend Him. Our entire wardrobe should commend Him. Would the length of your skirt commend Him? Would the color of your suit commend Him? Would the height of your heels commend Him? Would the condition of your teeth or dental work commend Him? Would your favorite jewelry and your favorite fragrance commend Him?

In other words, can it be said by those observing you that your appearance, at all times and in all ways, commend you as an Ambassador for Christ? That is the important question that must always remain alive in the mind and heart of a child of God.

Why do we, as believers, stand back and let the world dictate our appearance; tell us what's in vogue and what's out of fashion? I once heard a female caller to a radio program profoundly state that *"Women who are in vogue are often vague."* In other words, we're so focused on the outside that we fail to pay attention to what the Holy Spirit is whispering on the inside, regarding our outward appearance, as well as all that concerns us. And yet, the godly counsel of the Holy Spirit should always be our first and last consideration.

When my brothers and I were growing up, our parents and grandparents modeled before us each day, usually without saying a word, the importance of a godly appearance at all times. Long before I became a first year law student and learned that, pursuant to the rights and privileges contained in the First Amendment of the United States Constitution, our dress can be considered speech, I had already learned that from Mother, Mama, and Daddy at our home on Lillie Street in the Central Ward of Newark.

We, as believers, owe it to the Master to ask ourselves each day, before we leave our dwelling places, "Does my appearance command the approval of the crowd or does my appearance commend Christ?"

Stop Trying To Be Jesus, Jr.

Our time here on earth is so designed that, at specific times, certain individuals will cross our path or we shall cross theirs. It is God who puts us on our separate paths and allows paths to cross. Sometimes the crossing has been designed to use us as channels to meet the other person's need, enabling and encouraging them to go on.

What first appears as the chance meeting is nothing less than a divinely designed encounter. At those times when we are meeting the needs of another, be they spiritual or material, we must remember that God has ordained the occasion to give us the opportunity to point our fellow traveler to the Father. The child of God is merely the Father's appointed vessel through which the needed supply arrives.

If we are not careful to stay humbly in tune with the Father's desire for our specific use in the Kingdom, we shall fall into the trap of trying to be Jesus, Jr. to those in our midst that are in need. They may be family members, friends, co-workers or even strangers. We are not, cannot, and must not try to be Jesus, Jr. to our loved ones and other fellow travelers.

Jesus said, *"When you have seen me, you've seen the Father"* (John 14:9). Therefore, when we try to be Jesus, Jr., we are trying to be God. Only God can be God. There is only one Father, one Son and one Holy Spirit.

When we come across fellow travelers trying to navigate the deep waters of life, the greatest gift we can give them is our unashamed sharing of the Gospel of Jesus Christ. The Word of God promises us that every resource of every kind is stockpiled and available for our use. However, this avalanche of blessings can only be released at the throne of grace where we humbly make our prayer requests for help in our time of need.

Someone has said, "Life is a banquet. But poor fools sit around starving to death." As children of God, we don't have to starve. Nor do we have to take responsibility to keep others from starving, unless we are directed to do so by God.

If we shall remain in never ceasing prayer, and devote quality time to reading and meditating on the Word of God, and trust and obey God at every turn in the road, God shall pour out his blessings upon us, so that we shall not have room to receive them.

No one has to be Jesus, Jr. to another, nor should we try. Our duty is to simply point others to the Master by our conduct, caring, and confession.

"What You Think of Me Is None of My Business"

Some years ago, I found myself intrigued by the title of Terry Cole Whitaker's national bestseller, *"What You Think of Me Is None of My Business."*

We have all been brought to the earth to carry out a very special mission for the Lord. Our individual service is a part of God's business in the world. If our business is not God's business, we shall end up like the prodigal son—living in a far country; far beneath our royal heritage, our specific calling, and our sacred station in life. If our daily business is not God's business, then God has no obligation to keep us alive.

There will be people in our life who have taken it upon themselves to pass judgment on us, our personality, our preferences and our passions. It could be a spouse, a parent, a sibling or other relatives, friends or colleagues. Now this certainly doesn't mean that we're beyond reproof or correction. But it takes prayerful communion with the Father to be able to distinguish between what are genuine loving observations of needed changes in our behavior, versus what is essentially an attack on the precious person that God has made in His image and for His glory.

The incomparable musician, Quincy Jones, recognized in December, 2006, on ABC News as their "Person of the Week," stated that his mentor, the late, great musical genius, Ray Charles, said: *"Not one drop of my self worth depends upon your opinion of me."* That sounds just like vintage Ray.

Too many of us have failed to live an authentic, creatively productive and fruitful life because we are so tuned into the loud voices of the self-appointed judges. We miss the still, quiet, whispering voice of the Holy Spirit. God does not compete with the running commentary of the world. He lets it run its course, all the while saying,

"And if it seem evil unto you to serve the Lord, choose you this day whom ye will serve; whether the gods which your fathers served that were on the other side of the flood, or the

gods of the Amorites, in whose land ye dwell: but as for me and my house, we will serve the Lord."

                                            Joshua 24:15

When we refuse or fail to acknowledge Him by acknowledging first His Son, in all our ways, He simply lets us experience the painful consequences of our ungodly ways.

What other people think of us is really none of our business because they cannot, nor will they ever have knowledge of all of the facts of God's will for our life. They are unable to know all of the circumstances that He permits us to endure; circumstances that are designed to spiritually mature and equip us to successfully fulfill our divine mission.

What other people think of us is really none of our business because other individuals have limited understanding and finite perception of the workings of the Lord. Moreover, God tells us in His word:

"For my thoughts are not your thoughts, neither are your ways my ways, saith the Lord."

"For as the heavens are higher than the earth, so are my ways higher than your ways, and my thoughts than your thoughts."

                                            Isaiah 55:8-9

To focus on the business of another is to waste precious God-given time that we shall never be able to recapture. It is also a veiled attempt, albeit involuntary, to usurp the sovereignty, power and presence of the Lord.

Our self-examination, at every step along the path, and at every fork in the road, should be one of "Am I living according to God's Will for my life? Does God approve of my daily conduct and conversation? Does He, especially, approve of the confessions of my ability, through Christ, to carry out the assignment that He marked out for me before He knit me together in my mother's womb?"

Daily I ask the Holy Spirit to remind me that what people think of me is none of my business. Further, I ask the Holy Spirit to remind me that what God thinks of me is my business, and my only business. My full-time occupation with each hour of every day is to handle my business in such a way that at the end of my life, God shall welcome me home with open arms and a greeting of "Well done, my good and faithful servant Barbara." I invite you to join me in receiving this eternal reward.

"Go To Your Grave With The Reputation You Set People Free"

The Rev. Dr. Chuck Swindoll has wisely exhorted us, in the Spirit of Christ, to "Go to your grave with the reputation you set people free." Nothing is more in keeping with the principles and practices of Jesus than setting other people free from every imaginable bondage: the bondage of fear and intimidation; the bondage of sickness and disease; the bondage of sin; the bondage of unforgiveness; the bondage of hatred and hostility; the bondage of envy and jealousy; the bondage of poverty; the bondage of pain and suffering.

We set other people free when we introduce them to Jesus, our Lord and Savior; Our Prince of Peace; our Friend that sticketh closer than a brother; our Wonderful Counselor, our Almighty Father, our Everlasting Father; our Rose of Sharon; our Lily of the Valley; our Rock in a Weary Land; our Wheel in the Middle of A Wheel; our Mighty Fortress; our Shield and Buckler, the Great "I AM" who promises to be whatever, whenever and wherever we need Him to be.

We set other people free when we encourage them to be all they are meant to be in the world. We set other people free when we forgive those who trespass against us and say all manner of evil about us for Thy Name's sake.

Most people yearn to be free, even spend quality time fighting to be free, but have no understanding as to how to achieve their personal freedom. These are folks that look to the world for the answers to their important questions and for the solutions to their pressing problems. If they look long enough, they are sure to find that the answers and solutions promulgated by the world are momentary in lasting value and without a firm foundation.

Let us commit, in search of the freedom that we all seek, to introduce the Master to one another, in the Name of the Father and of the Son and of the Holy Ghost. Amen.

God Has Already Factored In Our Failures

Sometimes I reflect on the peace and security I could have experienced during my times of failure, if I had known a simple, but profound, truth. That truth is that God has already factored our failures into His providential plan for our life.

It is important that we distinguish failure from defeat. Failure is God's opportunity to teach us what does not work and to show us how to avoid repeating the same mistakes. God uses failure as His laboratory to show us where we erred. Defeat, on the other hand, is failure that hasn't factored God into the equation. When we see ourselves as defeated, it is because, contrary to the wise counsel of scripture, we have *"leaned unto our own understanding"* (Proverbs 3:5).

We are afraid of failure for a number of reasons. The first and foremost of which is that we are afraid of being laughed at and ridiculed. We are afraid of having it said that our failure serves us right. Who do we think we are, anyway? How dare we reach so high? We are afraid of failure because failing hurts. We'd rather do nothing than to try something and fail. This is the stance of the faithless coward and not that of the authentic believer. The believer knows that without Christ, he can do nothing; but with Him, nothing shall be impossible to him. The coward, on the other hand, fails to factor in Christ, and relies on the limitations of his own resources.

Think of failure as the pangs of birth. We set our sights on our goal. We take the first step. We fall down because we have never learned to walk before. We get up and we try again. We have learned that falling down is not so bad after all. In fact, we're just not as afraid of falling down as we were the first time we were about to take our first step.

The next time you are about to take a step in the direction of a goal, see yourself as stepping inside the palm of the Father's mighty and magnificent hand. You might fall down, but you won't fall out of His hand. And even if you should somehow fall out of His hand, His other hand is there to catch you before you hit the ground.

"Worry Doesn't Empty Today of Its Trouble, But Tomorrow of Its Strength"

Corrie Ten Boom, in reflecting on her years of anguished imprisonment in the Nazi Concentration Camp at Auschwitz, is said to have once remarked: "*Worry doesn't empty today of its trouble, but tomorrow of its strength.*"

When I attended Rutgers University Law School in Newark, the nature of the law school process was such that my classmates and I would already have spent weeks deeply immersed into the Spring semester of the law school year, without knowing how well we had done on our final exams, or more importantly, whether or not we had passed all of our classes.

Nevertheless, we were expected to focus fully on our new courses and simply wait until the grades of each professor were posted on the bulletin board outside of the main office on the first floor of the building, a few feet from the main entrance.

If we were to master the material for each new class and complete our homework assignments, we could not afford to concentrate on the semester that was over. That was done. We were now being challenged to move on to new territory. In order to be fully focused on the new subject matter, we had to let the past pass. This was ours to do individually. Our professors and fellow classmates couldn't do it for us.

During those three years as a law student, I considered the experience of delayed exam results to be limited and unique to the process of law school. I have since realized that, if we are to succeed in any endeavor, we must be willing to seize the moment, give it all we can and then let it go. In addition, we must recognize that there will always be inevitable factors and circumstances beyond our control. When the moment is over, we must go forward to the next moment, for, in actuality, we are all here for just one moment more. If we remain prayerful and faithful, in time, the Holy Spirit broadens our understanding, as well as acceptance, of this spiritual reality.

The process of life requires taking hold and then letting go. It is going through the revolving door to the other side. It is resisting the urge to stop the door or slow it down. It is trusting the process of life to take us through safely to the other side. It is the faithful resolve not to get caught in closing doors. When I am tempted to worry about tomorrow, I take courage in Paul's admonition to the Philippians: *"Do not be anxious about anything"* (Phil. 4:6). And in 1 Peter 5:7, we are commanded to *"Cast all your anxiety on Him."*

I don't know if any of my fellow classmates ever worried, as I did, about the grades that would sooner or later be posted. They never said. However, we did talk to each other about why some professors were so slow—posting grades on the board as late as April of the spring semester—while others could be counted on to post their grades upon our return from Christmas vacation. Without saying it, nevertheless, we fully understood that it took all of our strength and stamina to keep up with the class attendance and assignments of the spring semester.

Years later, as a trial attorney, the years of my law school experience would serve me well. While waiting for a court to render its decision in a particular case, I would remind myself that I had done my best. My attention must now be fully focused on my other active cases and court matters at hand.

Years earlier as a worried freshman at Douglass College, my father counseled me: "After you've done your best, leave the rest." I have modified Daddy's good counsel that anchors me today, no matter what I'm facing: "After you've done your best, leave the rest in God's hands and rest." We must honor the Father in our resolve not to worry. Worry simply doesn't fit who we are as children of the Most High God.

Furnace Time

If you continue to live, you will have to periodically undergo some furnace time. These are usually times of financial hardship, the long term illness of a family member, the death of a loved one, some kind of unjust treatment or persecution, sickness and disease, the loss of a job, surprising betrayal, slanderous and libelous attacks on your character and reputation or perhaps some circumstance that tests the level of your faith in Almighty God.

In the Book of Daniel, the three Hebrew boys—Shadrack, Meshack and Abednego— were threatened with furnace time if they did not publicly reject their God and bow to the King. They refused and were thrown into the fiery furnace. (Daniel 3:14-21). Through these three Hebrew boys and their furnace time experience, God had a great and important lesson to teach generations to come.

The Scriptures tell us that the boys were thrown into the furnace. The King arose the next morning and ran to the furnace, expecting to see the remains of the Hebrew boys going up in smoke from their ashes. Instead, he saw the boys walking around in the furnace. But that's not all he saw. He saw a fourth person walking around in the furnace, and it appeared to be the Son of God. (Daniel 3:25)

Through this story of the Hebrew boys, God teaches us that sometimes we shall have to face life threatening situations that we shall not be able to escape. We will just have to go through and endure. But we never go through and endure alone. God is right there with us. He has our back, our front, and our sides. *He has His hand on the thermostat and His eye on the thermometer.*

He is a man that cannot lie. And He has promised to be with us and to never leave us. When He releases us from our furnace time, we shall come out wiser, stronger, and less fearful of the fiery furnaces that still await us. We shall come out humbled, obedient and courageous. We shall come out knowing that this is not our battle; and the only fight we have to fight is the fight of faith. We shall come out richer in the things of God, knowing that it is He Who gives us every good and perfect gift. We shall know, more than ever before, that our God can be counted on to stand with us before the world's tribunals.

Therefore, we don't have to renounce our God, or sell our souls, to escape the fiery furnaces that are sure to come up every now and then. All we have to do is stand our ground, knowing that the Son of God is standing there with us.

The Holy Spirit will control the furnace makers, the temperature of the fire, and the length of time we have to stay in the furnace. But most of all, the Holy Spirit will see to it that we are not consumed by the fire. Further, He shall see to it that when we exit the furnace, not even the smell of smoke will be on us. We shall suddenly realize that the only thing that got burned up in the furnace were the shackles that had been placed on our feet and hands.

We can say, as did Daniel, to the powers that be: *"If it be so, our God whom we serve is able to deliver us from the burning fiery furnace, and he will deliver us out of thine hand, O King"* (Daniel 3:17).

The Holy Spirit Plays Be Bop

Through my younger brother, Tyrone Washington, child prodigy, musical genius, and noted American Jazz Musician, the Holy Spirit played Be Bop. To Jazz connoisseurs and others, Tyrone is not only warmly recognized around the world, but his music is sold in such far away places as Beijing, Dubai, Hong Kong, Singapore, India, Bangkok and Tokyo. His global recognition, through the Internet sale of his music, was surprisingly brought to my attention by one of my nieces a few years ago. I was also pleasantly surprised to learn that he and his music is, even now, the subject of Internet chat room conversations.

Each of us comes into the world at birth equipped by God with certain unique gifts and talents. When I recently proposed to my ten year old grandson, Jean-Pierre Perry (affectionately known as "J.P." by his family, friends and classmates), that if he were on television, he could make millions through the use of his God-given intellectual gifts, he quickly responded that "*We're not here to make millions, we're here to make a difference.*" How right he is.

God has designed us to achieve the "square of life" which consists of health, wealth, love and perfect self-expression by developing fully our innate and unique gifts and talents; and in so doing, make a needed difference in the world. Each individual has been brought into the world to do what no one else can do and be what no one else can be. And to reiterate the observation made by the late Dr. Benjamin E. Mays, former President of Morehouse College, my late husband's Alma Mater, and quoted earlier in the book: "*Every man is born into the world to do something unique and something distinctive, and if he or she does not do it, it will never be done.*"

Tyrone is an illustration of this eternal truth. He was born into our family gifted and anointed with an unusual musical ear and musical talent. From the time he was four or five years old, everyone recognized that he was born with music in his spirit, mind and soul. Whether the sounds were coming from the radio, the record player or the television, he responded with rapt attention, head bopping, fingers snapping and singing, or humming to the tune or lyrics.

From his early childhood, music and the self-mastery of musical instruments dominated his life. Tyrone began playing the piano before he could read. He later taught himself to play, with mastery, the piano, saxophone, flute, bass and drums. Actually, I don't know of any instrument that he couldn't play if he wanted to. Tyrone not only lived and breathed music; his music was for him his breath of life. There was never a dispute that he had been called by God to express his musical talents. Years later, my grandmother reminded me that she had tried to sponsor Tyrone in taking music lessons. But after a few lessons, Mama said that the music teacher advised the family to wait a while longer, since at that time Tyrone had not begun to read.

During visits with family members, Tyrone connected with his music. One afternoon while visiting with me in our apartment in East Orange, New Jersey, Tyrone asked if he could use my telephone. I said of course. When he picked up the telephone receiver, he swirled around and asked, "Barbara, did you know that your dial tone is A Minor? I said, "No, I didn't." On another visit to our home in Plainfield, New Jersey, Tyrone went onto the back porch and began to play his flute. He played so beautifully that one of my neighbors across the street wandered into our back yard and said that she had to come over and see where these wonderful musical sounds were coming from.

Following his graduation from Arts High School in Newark, Tyrone enrolled as a student at Howard University School of Music in Washington, D.C. While an undergraduate student at Howard, his classmate from Arts High School, the late Jazz Trumpeter, Woody Shaw, informed him that Horace Silver was looking for a saxophonist for his band and encouraged Tyrone to audition for the spot. Tyrone auditioned and was recruited by Horace Silver to join his band. Tyrone traveled around the world with The Horace Silver Quartet, playing Jazz. Tyrone is recognized in the music world and around the globe for having recorded such Jazz Classic Albums as *Roots, Natural Essence* and *Do Right*, just to name a few.

Sometime after I began working on Capitol Hill, I had a conversation with one of the Committee staffers. She shared with me her recollection of Tyrone as a fellow music major at Howard University. She recalled that one day the various music students had, one by one, come out of their individual music practice rooms to ask "Who is that?" They, of course, were referring to Tyrone working his musical magic on a grand piano. She said that from that point on, all the music students recognized Tyrone as having an extraordinary musical gift.

But it takes my daughter, Regan, to tell the story of an experience she had while an undergraduate at Spelman College. During her music professor's review of the course material prior to the final exam, he asked the class of young women what would be the correct answer to the question on the exam, "What was the name of the noted Alto Jazz Saxophonist (referring to Tyrone) who was a member of the Horace Silver Band?" The girls, in unison, answered: "Regan's uncle!" My nieces and nephews always love being reminded of this story.

The musical genius possessed by my brother is symbolic of the unique genius that resides within each individual through the indwelling of the Holy Spirit. Tyrone's individual and unique expression of his God-given musical talent, manifesting as Be Bop, is symbolic of the outworking of the Holy Spirit in us when we surrender to His call, and allow ourselves to be used as vessels to pour out His Spirit in the earth. Each of us, in some area of life, is a genius in our own right, representing the indwelling of the Holy Spirit that desires to do a new thing through us; that seeks an outworking of some unique gift and talent that cannot be expressed by anybody but us.

It is the Holy Spirit, and not we ourselves, that enables us to minister with our unique gift to the entire world. *Without Him, we can do nothing. With Him, we can do all that God has designed us to be, do and have.* He resides in us, empowering us, enabling us, providing for us, protecting us, and strengthening us to do the work that the Father has called us to do on His behalf as His representatives.

Our responsibility, through prayer and meditation, is to become acquainted and comfortable with our God-given gifts and talents; and God's ordained will for their specific expression and use in the world. And, depending on your divine gifts, and God's plan and purpose for your life, don't be surprised if the Holy Spirit chooses to play Be Bop, or its divine equivalent, through you, too!

In 1968, Tyrone accepted Islam as his religion and became known as Muhammad Bilal Abdullah.

When You Want To Scream,
Take A Deep Breath And Exhale A Prayer

One of the ways Satan likes to keep followers of Christ from carrying out their God-given assignment is to put tremendous pressure on them from every direction. His ultimate goal is to put so much pressure on the child of God that he becomes a screaming, babbling idiot before the world. The child of God becomes nothing less than an embarrassment, if you will, to the Kingdom of God.

Through faith in Christ, we can overcome the vile attacks of the enemy without breaking down and without destroying our witness before a watching world.

One proven method that serves well in resisting the Enemy and that will enable us to take a firm stance against the unrelenting, vicious attacks of the Enemy sounds simple, but works. It is a method that is perfectly suitable for us, or members of our family, when we are experiencing a season of being under siege by the Enemy. Throughout the day, or if you should awaken during the night, and are tempted (by Satan, of course) to scream, take a deep breath and exhale a prayer. You might be saying, "Is that all?" And my testimony and witness to you is, "That is all."

And believe me, it works. The reason it works is because when we pray, even second or minute prayers, we are not only talking and listening to the Lord, we are battling with the Devil.

When I have been under the most intense onslaught of the Enemy, what has saved me from just throwing up my hands and screaming are my favorite exhaled prayers. They are the following: "Help me, Lord." "Strengthen me, Jesus." "Give me your wisdom, Father." "Give me the right idea, Lord." "Thank you, Father." "Protect me Father." and "Favor me, Lord." The exhaled prayer that I say more than any other is "Thy will be done." This is the prayer of surrender. Surrender to what? Surrender to the perfect plan and purpose of God for my life. It is the prayer that warms God's heart and makes Him smile.

As a child of God, you don't have to scream when you can pray to the Father. Your Father is calling all the shots, pulling all the strings and controlling everything in the world, including Satan. In fact, Satan is just a mere pawn in the plan of God for your life. In fact, I like the description of Satan's engagements made by the Rev. Dr. Tony Evans, Senior Pastor of Oak Cliff Bible Fellowship and President of The Urban Alternative: *"On his best day, Satan is achieving the plan and purpose of God."* Try to remember that the next time he sends his fiery darts your way.

However and whenever you are being pressured, beyond what you think you can bear, take a deep breath, exhale a prayer and then relax in the loving arms of Jesus. Over time, you will look back and be astounded at the wonderful results God has wrought.

"God Is Looking For Iron Saints"

Perhaps you are familiar with the Bible story of Joseph and his coat of many colors. He was sold into slavery by his older brothers, motivated by their intense and evil jealousy of him, the special attention he received from his Father, Jacob, and his dreams that foretold that one day he would rule over his brothers and their Father.

Psalm 105:18 (NIV) tells us that, "*His neck was put in irons.*" Depending on how familiar you are with the story, you know that God took Joseph from slavery, to prison, and finally to the palace as Prime Minister, after thirteen long years of pain and suffering, ostensibly caused by his envious brothers. But Joseph knew that the real Cause of his suffering and pain that made up the circuitous route to the position of Prime Minister over all of Egypt was his Omnipotent God.

When his brothers appeared before him, begging for bread, and totally unaware of his identity, Joseph, following in the footsteps of Christ, set the example of how we must treat those who have committed even the most heinous acts against us. After revealing his true identity to his brothers, Joseph told them:

"*Come closer to me," Joseph said to his brothers.*
They came closer. "I am Joseph your brother whom you sold into Egypt. But don't feel badly, don't blame yourselves for selling me. God was behind it. God sent me here ahead of you to save lives. There has been a famine in the land now for two years; the famine will continue for five more years— neither plowing nor harvesting. God sent me on ahead to pave the way and make sure there was a remnant in the land, to save your lives in an amazing act of deliverance. So you see, it wasn't you who sent me here but God. He set me in place as a father to Pharaoh, put me charge of his personal affairs, and made me ruler of all Egypt." (Genesis 45:4-8 NIV).

As L.B. Cowman tells us: "God is looking for iron saints;" saints that can withstand the inevitable pressures and storms of life. The Master is looking for saints that can "take a licking and keep on ticking."

If we are to carry out our God-given assignments, we must be persons of iron will and strength. God allows His saints to suffer because, through suffering, God instills the tenacity, fortitude, endurance, steadfastness, patience, persistence and strength of purpose that are needed to follow Christ.

It is the saint of iron will and strength that is able to withstand the scorn and ridicule of others, opposition on every hand, affliction, misunderstandings, false accusations and the garden variety of satanic attacks. See your suffering as the Holy Spirit's process of putting you through circumstances that allow iron to enter your soul to make you fearless and faithful. God knows the best ways of instilling iron into our spiritual life. We must resist the temptation to second-guess or question His ways. It is the spiritual life instilled with iron that is able to stand firm and not be overcome by the onslaught of the Enemy no matter what form or how long it lasts.

"Dripping Water Will Wear Stone Away"

Daddy died suddenly and unexpectedly. He suffered a stroke on Tuesday and was gone by Thursday. The loss of my father was the first deep loss I would experience as an adult. I was emotionally numbed by the overwhelming grief, and would remain so for approximately a whole year. Nevertheless, I knew that I had to go on. I also knew that God was with me. More importantly, I knew with the author of a greeting card message that *"if God brings you to it, He will bring you through it."*

Yes, Daddy was gone, but his spirit and his words would be forever with me. When I reflect on my childhood, I now realize that Daddy, Mother and Mama taught us almost exclusively by the example of their lives they lived before us; and by their use of graphic metaphors.

For example, I don't ever remember Daddy telling me to be persistent in my pursuit of some goal that appeared to be beyond my reach. Rather, Daddy would say, *"Always remember, dripping water will wear stone away."* What better description of persistence than dripping water? Dripping water is constant. It's continuous. It doesn't let up. It can be aggravating, if not annoying. It drips in sunshine and in rain; whether it's hot or cold; whether we're at war or peace; whether the Democrats or Republicans are in office; whether you're experiencing loss or gain; whether you're sick or well; whether you have a job or you're out of work; and in good times or so-called bad times. And then, on top of Daddy's classic admonition, I would remember Elizabeth Barrett Browning's pensive query: *"If your goal doesn't exceed your reach, then what's a heaven for?"*

A poem entitled "Press On" is engraved on a plaque that hangs on my kitchen cabinet. Its words are as follows:

> "Nothing in the world can take
> the place of persistence.
> Talent will not.
> Nothing is more common than
> unsuccessful men with talent.

Genius will not.
Unrewarded genius is almost a proverb.
Education will not.
The world is full of educated derelicts.
Persistence and determination alone are omnipotent."

Daddy's "dripping water theology" joins in spirit, if not in words, with that of the unknown author of this poem. It is persistence, more than any other factor, which determines the achievement and mastery of our goals.

Thank you, Daddy.

Never Fret Or Become Upset
Over Your Circumstances

No matter what you're going through, God is in absolute control over your circumstances. All your circumstances. Every detail of every circumstance. Therefore, in the words of a believer, and as a child of God, you need "Never become extremely upset over your circumstances." God has made a promise in His word to every child of God that *"He causes all things to work together for good to those that love the Lord and are called according to His purpose"* (Romans 8:28).

God is a Man who does not lie. He is also the Man that died for you. As another believer has shared, *"You can trust the Man who died for you."* Your circumstances, no matter how painful or unwanted, have been arranged, or if not arranged, allowed by God. From the Master's perspective, your circumstances are sacred and sealed in His unconditional love for you.

If God has given the nod to our circumstances, we must yield to His will. It is the foolish man or woman, boy or girl, who tries to second-guess God. We are no match for our Maker. He made us and He knows all about us. As the old Gospel song reminds us, *"He knows just how much we can bear."* But He also knows what it will take to prepare us for maximum service in the Kingdom of God.

For one believer it might take the loss of a job to give him the special attribute he'll need in his unique role in the Kingdom. For another, it might take the infidelity of a spouse, the betrayal of a dear friend, the abandonment by one's family, or the loss of one that was dearly loved.

When we allow ourselves to fret or become upset over our circumstances, what we communicate is that God is obviously not in absolute control. Our fretful disturbance over our circumstances says to the world that we serve a God whose sovereignty is limited and qualified. To a watching world, we leave ourselves open to be read as individuals who serve a God of limited power and authority.

God can only do for us what He can do through us. And He can only do through us what we allow Him to do. This is not just a circuitous assertion. This is how God works. In Isaiah 45:11, God extends to each believer an unlimited and unqualified invitation. He tells us "...*concerning the work of my hands, command ye me.*" Very simply, God is saying, "Tell me what you want me to do for you."

God knows that there will be times when our situation will all but overwhelm us. These are times when He wants us to not fret or become upset over our circumstances; but to look to Him for whatever is needed to assume a firm stance right in the midst of our troubling circumstances.

When it comes to fretting or becoming upset over our circumstances, no one models more what our reaction should be, as children of God, than the Apostle Paul. He tells us in no uncertain terms in Philippians 4:11 "...*for I have learned in whatever state I am, therewith to be content.*" Daddy made a point of reminding me of this scripture when he was aware of those times in my life when the very gates of hell were trying to prevail against me.

Paul's commitment to be content in all circumstances speaks volumes of his trust in the Almighty God and His Son, Jesus Christ. We have evidence of the truth of Paul's statement. When he was imprisoned, rather than bemoaning his painful condition of incarceration, or hurling curses at his jailers, Paul and Silas sang songs of praise and thanksgiving to their Father on high. Paul recognized that his circumstances were being orchestrated and controlled by the Almighty God. Paul did not fret nor become upset over his circumstances. Paul was not moved by his circumstances. Therefore, his circumstances had to move.

The Books You Read, The Places You Go, The People You Meet

Significant in our spiritual development is God's use of certain temporal resources to serve as our teachers, classrooms and laboratories. These resources have been divinely designed by God to provide us with learning experiences that uniquely equip us to fulfill our God-given assignment in the world. Moreover, they eternally impact the nurturance of our very souls.

The resources that I refer to can be grouped in one of three categories. They are *the books you read, the places you go, and the people you meet.* However they arrive in your life, I consider these three resources to be straight from the Father's hand.

There is no question that the contents of a book can deeply impact your life. Witness the millions, if not billions, of people whose lives have been impacted by the Bible. I don't remember when I did not have a natural affection, if not obsession, with books. As a child growing up in the City of Newark, I cherished our neighborhood branch of the Newark Public Library. It was my second home away from home.

As a student at the Eighteenth Avenue Elementary School, I spent most of my hours after school, reading books and viewing photographs of foreign capitols around the world that I dreamed of visiting one day. Since we were always encouraged by our parents and grandparents to dream and dream big, I never doubted for one moment, while sitting in the library, that one day I would visit the exotic places that I could now only dream about. After all, did we not sing regularly in church service the old gospel song whose lyrics stated, in part, "The Lord will make a way somehow?"

Long before I entered Barringer High School, I cherished books almost as much as I cherished my family, my relationship with Jesus, and our church. Consequently, I have never forgotten the invaluable advice given to our senior class one day by one of my favorite teachers, Mr. Pat Restaino. In addressing those of us in the class who would not be going on to college after graduation, but would nevertheless benefit from a college education, Mr. Restaino suggested that we commit to reading at least three different books a week. I have never forgotten this teaching on the important role of books in one's life.

At the age of sixteen, and still a student at Barringer High School, God rewarded my years of library study and persistent visualization of overseas travel in a most magnificent way. Two of my history teachers—Ms. Lucille Augustus and Dr. Halperin—each approached me separately at school one day, and gave me an application form for an essay contest being offered to public high school students in the City of Newark. Little did I realize at the time that this experience, more than any other, would sum up for me the deep impact made on a person's life by the combination of the books they read, the places they go and the people they meet.

The contest was sponsored by the Newark Chapter of the American Association for the United Nations. The essay contestants were asked to tell why they would qualify as an outstanding American Youth Goodwill Ambassador. The prize was an all expense paid 56-Day-Trip-Around-the-World. Two winners would be selected from the final contestants. The student winners would be accompanied by an official chaperone. They would travel around the world as American Youth Goodwill Ambassadors. Their itinerary included visits to seventeen foreign countries in Europe, the Middle East, Asia and the Far East. The trip would take place in the months of July and August, and the students and their chaperone would return to the States in September.

Since I was told of the contest and given an application from not one, but two of my favorite teachers, I interpreted this to be, if nothing else, certainly an auspicious sign regarding my contest participation. I officially entered the contest and wrote the best essay that I could. After the judges' reading and evaluation of the many essays submitted by students across the city, I was selected as one of five contest finalists. Ultimately, two winners were selected from the group of five finalists—one female and one male.

However, following the announcement of the two winners, surprisingly there was an unexpected outpouring of public interest and support that all five finalists, a more racially representative group, should be sponsored and travel abroad as American Youth

Goodwill Ambassadors. Thereafter, donations poured in from around the city and throughout the region of predominant metropolitan Essex County. The fundraising effort was successful, making it possible for all of the five finalists to circle the globe as American Youth Goodwill Ambassadors.

In preparation for our trip, we were briefed in New York City by American diplomats and the late Mrs. Eleanor Roosevelt. We were given a marvelous send-off including front page coverage in the "Newark Evening News" newspaper as we prepared for boarding. We were met by American and foreign diplomats when we landed at the airport of each foreign capitol. Although unofficial, we were always treated and regarded by our international hosts and hostesses as official American diplomats visiting their country.

We would spend our days meeting with the youth leaders, city officials and members of the diplomatic community in each country. We would then return to our hotel and spend our time getting dressed for dinner while watching ourselves on the evening news. For example, I shall always remember our meeting, as "Youth Ambassadors," with the then Prime Minister of Thailand, His Excellency, Kittikachorn, in the Royal Palace. We reveled in seeing ourselves that evening on television being greeted by the political leader of Thailand.

Those fifty-six (56) days abroad changed my life for the rest of my life. I was certain that God had rewarded me for the faithfulness and obedience to His Word that I had exhibited since the early age of six or seven years old. It was at that time that I walked, alone, down the aisle of the St. Luke A.M.E. Church, located on Prince Street in Newark, and formally gave my life to Christ. I pledged to follow Him, wherever He would lead me for the rest of my life.

I was never again to be intimidated by persons of high rank, either because of their great wealth or powerful position in the world. When the temptation of the world would come calling, I would remember that God had already shown me the entire world at the age of sixteen and, at the level of an ambassador, albeit a Youth Ambassador. The experience humbled me as a follower of Christ. It confirmed for me, for all time, that God can and will do exceedingly, abundantly above all that we could ever ask or dream.

"If You Catch Hell Don't Keep It"

We are helpless and powerless, without the aid of our Almighty God, to resist Satan in all of his many destructive designs and disguises.

Sometimes his costume of the day is a fast ball thrown our way. It appears at first glance to be a blessing. But since it is rushing our way, we fail to make the fine distinctions necessary in confrontation with the Enemy. He characteristically and intentionally surrounds us with an atmosphere of "Hurry up. You won't get this chance again." He carefully omits telling you that only God has the best plan for your life.

Satan's fast balls are designed exclusively to harm us in some way. Demonic fast balls come solidly packed to kill, steal and destroy us. They are made to render our service in the Kingdom of God null and void. Therefore, we must drop these demonic fast balls as soon as we catch them. "Drop them while they're hot." If you have difficulty dropping the fast ball, then ask God to give you the strength, or whatever it takes to do so, and He will.

Anger, bitterness, envy, and covetousness are the fast balls made and thrown our way by the Devil. Other fast balls laying around Satan's pitcher's mound and designed to strike you out are fear, despair, disappointment, greed and moral depravity of every kind.

Satan's goal is to get us out of the game—pronto. He wants to extinguish our light, cripple our holy walk and convert our faith confession to murmuring, doubting and complaining. What distinguishes persons of faith from unbelievers is what we do with the fast ball when it's in our hand.

The choice is always ours. Once we see hell's fast ball being hurled our way, we have one of two choices. We can catch hell's fast ball and keep it. If we keep it, we keep all the misery that comes with hellish circumstances. Or we can faithfully and obediently cast whatever Satan sends our way onto Him who is able to do exceedingly, abundantly above all we could ever ask, think or dream.

When we catch one of hell's fast balls, it is our manifold duty to remember that we are *"more than conquerors through Him who loved us"* (Romans 8:37).

Therefore, *"If you catch hell, don't keep it."*

That Boat Sailed

Nothing is more untrue than the social adage: "Opportunity knocks once." A more accurate statement would be *"Opportunity knocks again and again. She just arrives in different attire and at different times."*

Periodically in life, we are faced with the circumstance of having to admit that by the time we arrive at the dock, the boat the Father had designed and scheduled for us to board has already sailed. I also sometimes refer to this situation as having stayed too long at the fair. Because of our fear of the great unknown, we hold tightly to what we can see and know. Whereas, opportunity time requires that we take those risks that are impressed upon our hearts by the Holy Spirit in response to regular, concentrated prayer and meditation in the Word of God.

Our challenge at this time is not to despair, but to prepare. Our life is not limited to one boat of opportunity. Our God is a God of repeated chances. His resources are unlimited. He has boats of opportunity "pressed down, shaken together and running over."

Your boat that sailed could be a job or business opportunity that you failed to pursue. Not to worry. Another one is already on its way to your dock. Or, your missed boat could be a right relationship or answer to prayer that you did not recognize as such, and so let it sail by.

However you define your missed opportunity, it is time to acknowledge, *"That boat sailed."* Even as you read these words, there are many more boats sailing your way. Your sacred duty to your Divine mission in life is to make haste and prepare for these opportunities.

Rest assured, sooner than you think, the next boat of opportunity will pull into your dock. And when it does, be prepared to step onto the gangplank to your Divine destination. Be prepared to step into your promised land.

Cruising All Over Heaven

One night, about two months after Mama had gone home to Glory, I saw Mama in a dream. She was way off in the distance, driving a big, beautiful, black limousine. And then she was gone.

There was no doubt in my mind that Mama's spirit came to tell me that Mama has finally overcome her fear of driving cars that she had while here on earth. During all of my life, I had not once remembered Mama desiring to drive or having a driver's license. Daddy had always transported Mama to work, to church on Sundays and to her grocery shopping.

After Daddy passed, Mama would take buses to wherever she wanted to go. One of her delights was leaving work, taking a bus to downtown Newark, and stopping by "the 5 & 10 Cent Store" which everyone called Woolworth's Department Store. She would have something to eat at the lunch counter, browse through the store and take the bus home to Fairmount Avenue, which was only a 10 to 15 minute ride on the bus.

Mama rode the public service buses to and fro and around town in the sunshine and rain, sleet and snow, foggy and bright, hot and cold, windy and balmy weather. She wagged with her bags, never complaining, never blaming, never depressed; always praising others, always caring for others, always giving to others, always blessing others; always giving praise to her Lord and Savior, Jesus Christ.

I am overjoyed to know that my Mama is now chauffeuring herself around Heaven all day. She doesn't have to wait anymore for public transportation. In my dream, Mama was leaning slightly to her left, with one hand on the steering wheel, cruising all over Heaven.

The Judas Experience

The Judas Experience refers to the profound betrayal that we suffer as a consequence of placing our faith, trust and confidence in another person who subsequently betrays our trust.

Jesus considered Judas to be one of his closest friends and companions. However, it was Judas that told the Pharisees and Roman soldiers where Jesus could be found so that they could arrest Him. The Bible informs us, *"Now he that betrayed him gave them a sign, saying, whomsoever I shall kiss, that same is he: hold him fast"* (Matthew 26:48). And it was the arrest of Christ that led to his being nailed to the cross, the scorning, mockery, and jeering of the crowd; the crucifixion, death, birth and resurrection from the grave on the third day.

The Judas Experience is meant to teach us the lesson that foolish is the man or woman who puts their faith and confidence in another human being to treat them fairly and equitably, to treat them justly. The only real justice resides in the power of the Almighty. Judas' betrayal of Jesus teaches us that it is divine justice that rules and overrules in the mix of human experience. Betrayal in the life of a child of God is just one step further along the path of our ultimate fulfillment of our divine assignment.

No matter how much we are hurt, we must see betrayal for what it is—a piece of the tapestry of God's plan and purpose for our life. If we commit to seeing betrayal, in all its many forms, from God's perspective, we shall be able to prayerfully endure the pain and disappointment that goes with it. This takes great trust and faith in the unconditional love of the Father.

We must look to the model of our eldest brother, Jesus, and see betrayal as coming directly from the hands of the Father. And if the Father sends it, we must bow down and suffer it, knowing that God has uniquely engineered our betrayal to conform us to the individually tailored resurrected life that only we can live to His honor and glory.

The appearance of Judas in the life of the Believer is the divine initiation of the process that has been orchestrated by the Holy Spirit.

200

It is designed to catapult the child of God from the anonymity of every day life to the cross of redemption. It is marked by the isolation and silence of the grave that ultimately leads to the mystery, mastery and power of the resurrection in Christ Jesus.

And so when Judas appears in our lives, we must resolve to submit to God, stand firm in the face of the betrayal of the moment, and not run away from the lies, false accusations, attacks, slander, and social shunning. We shall look up one day and see that God has somehow, through His infinite wisdom, power and mercy, rolled the stone away from our personal tomb. We shall then be free to walk the path of Emmaus and feel our hearts burn within us.

Judas will always be symbolic of betrayal, deception and intended destruction of the God that is within us. Jesus, our elder brother, is our model for our resolve in the face of the most brutal betrayal to obey God and to leave all the consequences to Him.

No human plan will ever preempt the divine plan. All human plans of betrayal must inevitably bow to the divine plan of justice and order that prevails in the universe.

Both Judas and Jesus had historical roles given to them by their Maker. Judas carried out his role and then committed suicide. Jesus carried out his role and then ascended into Heaven. There He now sits at the right hand of the Father, forever interceding, even on behalf of those who still cry, "Crucify Him."

"God Don't Like Ugly, And He Ain't Too Crazy About Pretty"

Mama always had her own language made up of her own unique idioms, pet phrases, metaphors and similes. Most of Mama's speech was biblically based. In some way, her words always referenced God, Jesus, the Holy Ghost or all three at once. Mama was never intimidated by the grammatical rules of English or the vicissitudes of verbal jousting that often characterizes every day conversational English.

I have never met anyone, even in the highest halls of academia, that could outmatch or outmaneuver Mama in her skills as a great communicator. She had a way with words that was unique and riveting to the listener. Mama had a mastery of the English language that always astounded me, even though her formal education did not go beyond the eighth grade.

Mama also seemed to have her own built-in lie detector system. Say what you wanted to her, in any form or fashion —she knew intuitively when the truth being presented was not *the truth, the whole truth and nothing but the truth.* On top of that, even before her cataract surgery on both eyes, Mama's 20/20 vision had matured over the years to that of the 20/20 vision of at least three people. She had eagle eyes. Mama could see a storm coming long before the weatherman was able to forecast it.

She was always able to accurately, precisely and concisely evaluate other people's stuff right on the spot. If something was worrying you and you shared it with Mama; after hearing you out, she would say, "Oh, you can put your mind on something else, because that ain't nothin' to worry about." Sure enough, days, weeks or months later, you'd see that what previously had you tossing and turning at night, turned out to be nothing— just as Mama had called it. Mama not only saw the fault in our character and the error of our ways, she had the guts, courage and hudspeth to call it as she saw it. She didn't back down from anybody.

Mama knew that the only way we were going to be blessed by God with *"pressed down, shaken together and running over"* bless-

ings would be if we were obedient to God's commandments, and if we were willing to renounce our natural escapist inclinations in the face of Christ-centered crucibles, however unbeknownst to us, that the Divine Designer had tailor-made just for us.

And so when we were disobedient in any shape or form in Mama's presence, she would evenly and firmly say, looking directly into our eyes, if not into our very souls, and with all the accompaniment of heaven backing her up, *"God don't like ugly, and He ain't too crazy about pretty."* Mama, Mother and Daddy had taught us effectively that God frowns upon our disobedience. They also taught us that even when we think that we are pleasing to God, we must still remember that *"He ain't too crazy about pretty."*

Thank you, Mama.

Pontius Pilate

In the New Testament Scriptures, the story is told of Jesus' arraignment before Pontius Pilate. Pilate begins to question Jesus. And the Scriptures state that Jesus said not a word. Finally, in exasperation, Pilate asks Jesus, "...Speakest thou not unto me? Knowest thou not that I have power to crucify thee, and have power to release thee?" (John19:10).

And then sweet Jesus gives the answer of all answers. He gives what can be considered the model answer to be used by the child of God when faced with a challenge or temptation of the Enemy.

Jesus' classic, ready response was "...*Thou couldest have no power at all against me, except it were given thee from above: therefore he that delivered me unto thee hath the greater sin*" (John 19:11). In other words, you only have power because my Father gives it to you. In one sentence, Jesus spoke truth to power. In essence, Jesus said to Pontius Pilate, "Mr. Pilate, you do not scare me. I answer to one power and one power only. And that power is my Father. Your power is subject to the authority of my heavenly Father. My Father has given Satan permission to use you in the exercise of this demonic power."

Jesus was making it clear that He was not going to bow to the power of Pilate or any other flesh and bones human being. Jesus, at that moment, resolved to pay the ultimate price of His very life. He chose the death of crucifixion, trusting that God would raise Him up on the third day.

Jesus surrendered all to Him that is able to bring Him through the crucifixion to the dawn of the new day of the resurrection. Jesus, in that moment of brief dialogue with Pilate, cast His human fear aside and looked beyond Pilate to the Power that is sovereign; the power that is the great "I AM" in the midst of our time of need.

If we are followers of Jesus, we shall repeatedly suffer trials and persecutions. We shall be brought before the Pontius Pilates of our day and community. The faith challenge is to see these times before the earthly tribunals of power as special, if not sacred, opportunities. These are times when we must declare before the world, through our conduct, conversation and confession, that it is our Father that gives the world's Pilates power, in any form, over us.

Most of us, at one time or another have feared the furnace, the lions' den, or the cross. But there is no blessing greater than to realize one day that it has been in our furnaces, our lions' dens, our crosses that we have had the most spiritually transforming and freeing encounters with the Master.

The next time you are brought before this world's brand of Pontius Pilate, let the example of Jesus inspire you to understand that Pontius Pilate has not been put in your life to be feared, but as merely the next stop along the route to your ultimate resurrection in Christ Jesus.

Jesus brilliantly used His appearance before Pontius Pilate as a teaching moment. In a matter of seconds, Jesus had educated Pontius Pilate as to the real balance of power in the world. As a child of God, you, too, have been given power from on high. It is the power to stand before the world's tribunals and speak truth to power—the truth of the gospel of the Lord Jesus Christ.

"Play The Hand You're Dealt"

While living in India, I read a statement, reportedly made by Nehru, former Prime Minister of India. In describing his philosophy of life, Nehru was quoted as having declared "Play the hand you're dealt." Metaphorically, Nehru was obviously referring to the fact that when we are a participant in a card game, we are dealt certain cards by the dealer. The statement made a great impression upon me. Consequently, I've always remembered it.

At the time I came across the comment, we were living in Hyderabad, India as staff members of the American Peace Corps. My husband had been assigned there as an Associate Peace Corps Director. When we arrived, our daughter, Regan Alexandria, was still an infant. My role, although informal, entailed assisting my husband with all of the important social and political tasks assigned to him as a diplomatic officer. After about a year in Hyderabad, my husband was assigned to head the American Peace Corps Office in Patna, Bihar, formerly known as the famine state.

Metaphorically, life has a way of dealing us cards that sometimes are so shocking in their impact on our lives; they take our very breath away. When we participate in a card game, we are dealt certain cards by the dealer. As the card game opens, we witness the shuffling of the cards. This allows us the opportunity to see that the cards in the deck have not been intentionally stacked against us. The specific cards dealt us are not in our control. Nor are they within the control of the dealer, if they have been mixed and shuffled fairly. The ultimate challenge and even excitement of the card game is to know that if we are a skillful and shrewd card player, we can still come out the winner—no matter what hand we're dealt.

When we were growing up in Newark, our family was a member of the St. Luke A.M.E. Church. My brothers and I were very active in a variety of church clubs for children. One of the clubs that we were members of was the Junior Usher Board. Our club meeting was held once a month on a Saturday morning at the home of the church adult Club Leader—a senior usher. She was a veteran church member who also was a member of the Senior Usher Board. Her apartment was far from our house. Nevertheless, we would walk the whole way which was probably three miles or more. In those days, children in our neighborhood walked everywhere. We had nothing but time and the city was then considered safe for children to walk alone or together and travel way across town when necessary.

We would begin our business meeting in our Club Leader's living room. We would go over the status of our monthly dues and the status of our proper attire when on assignment as junior ushers in our church on the fourth Sunday of the month. The fourth Sunday of every month was the Sunday when the children and young people were in charge of the entire service. The meeting would open with a prayer and church hymn.

After the business meeting, our Club Leader always served some delicious snacks for us to eat. After we had feasted on the filling snacks, we would sit down in her kitchen and play cards. As far as I was concerned, and from my perspective, the card games were the most exciting part of the Junior Usher Board Meeting.

I remember winning some and losing some. I also remember being all smiles if I won and not as many smiles if I lost. But unhappy about losing? Not for a minute. My attitude was it's only a game. I can't win them all. And the fact that I lost at the last meeting didn't deter me at all from trying my hand at the next meeting—and with gusto.

I start out by believing, as Nehru, that life can be looked at as a card game. You can't control the cards that you're dealt, but you can control the way you play our hand. So, even if the cards are stacked against you and you, at times, feel backed into a corner, don't throw up your hands in exasperation and defeat, but play the hand you're dealt, and play to win anyway.

"It'll Be Over-In-A-Minute"

No matter what you may be going through, in the words of the dynamic Rev. Dr. Jackie McCullough, Senior Pastor of the International Gathering at Beth Rapha, *"It'll be over-in-a-minute."* These were the encouraging and inspiring words given by this anointed evangelist, Bible teacher and scholar to the hundreds of women in attendance during one of the evening services at our church's Annual Women's Retreat some years ago. My spirit and mind were so moved by her words that evening, and still are, that they will stay in my heart forever.

Perhaps your situation has gotten so painful that you're ready to end it all. You're ready to do something foolish. You're ready to do something that you'll regret for the rest of your life. Stop! Know that God has promised that, *"It'll be over-in-a-minute."*

My parents' and grandparents' generation had their own way of expressing this spiritual truth. They simply said, albeit ungrammatically, "Trouble don't last always."

Paul considered trouble as a "light affliction" that doesn't compare with our rewards in heaven. *"For our light affliction, which is but for a moment, worketh for us a far more exceeding and eternal weight of glory"*(2 Corinthians 4:17). And for Paul, this included being slandered and falsely accused, suffering insults and beatings; being shipwrecked and enduring unjust imprisonment.

As children of the Most High God, our Father expects us to view our troubles for what they really are: temporary trials and testing, orchestrated by God, to make us into men and women of perfect faith and godly character. While we will, on occasion, shed tears, David encourages us that *"Weeping may endure for a night, but rejoicing comes in the morning"* (Psalm 30:5).

When we view our troubles from God's eternal perspective, the Holy Spirit enlightens us to see through His eyes that trouble doesn't last always. Trouble comes to anoint us in our ability to carry out our divine assignment in the Kingdom. Once we see God's grace as more than sufficient for our troubles, then the trouble that has come must pass. Sifted through God's hands, trouble comes, not to punish us, but to prepare us for a blessing that is guaranteed to be pressed down, shaken together and so running over that there shall not be room enough to receive it (Luke 6:38; Malachi 3:10).

If, in the face of trouble, we refuse to give up, give in, or give out; if we resolve to trust God's heart, even when we can't trace His hand; if we, by faith, believe that God is always in sovereign and absolute control; then no matter by whom, what, where, when or why trouble appears, *"It'll be over-in-a-minute."*

Answered Prayer Takes Time

A rose in full bloom comes first packaged in a tiny seed. It takes time to shop for the seed. It takes time to plant the seed in the ground. It takes time to fertilize the ground; that is, to prepare the ground to receive, to the maximum benefit, the sunshine and rain. It takes time for clouds to form in the sky. It takes time for the rain to fall to the ground. We would readily agree that it takes time for the seasons to change.

It takes time for the sun to rise and to shine upon the ground that houses the seed underneath. It takes time for the sun to set at the end of another day. It takes time for the seed to take root, germinate and sprout above the ground. And in the midst of the germination and sprouting of the seed, God, in His infinite omnipotence and omniscience, is coloring the rose, albeit under cover. Consequently, "It takes time for God to color a rose" (Cowman, Op. Cit., p.161).

Just as it takes time for God to color a rose, *it takes time for God to answer prayer.* We pray to the Father. From the moment God hears our prayer, He begins to answer. And while we are praying to the Father in secret, the Father begins to answer our prayer openly, and for the entire world to see.

God uses channels and vessels too numerous to name or categorize. Sometimes God puts us on someone's mind to act as the channel of blessing from the Lord. Sometimes the answer to prayer comes in the form of favor extended to us by an authority figure. At other times, God causes our circumstances to make a complete about face with very little effort, if any at all, on our part.

Often our answer to a specific prayer takes the form of 1) the deepening of our faith in the sovereignty of God; 2) the increase in our resolve to be obedient to God's instructions to us; 3) the courage to leave all the consequences to Him; and 4) the spiritual maturity to see all the details of our circumstances and situations from God's perspective, which is one of unconditional love, infinite wisdom and sovereign control.

God has so designed the universe that waiting must be factored in as a necessary ingredient to answered prayer. From the moment we reach out to God in prayer, our prayer is the seed needed for God to color our rose, for God to answer our prayer.

Our timing is different from God's timing. When we are unwilling to wait on God to color our rose; when we dig up our seed sown in prayer; we further delay, if not derail altogether, the wonderful plans God has for our life.

"Escapist Inclinations"

We all find ourselves, periodically, in circumstances that we are inclined to want to escape. L.B. Cowman refers to this human phenomenon as our "escapist inclinations."

Problems, pain, pressure, angst, depression, bitterness, hostility, jealousy, unforgiveness, revenge, fear and intimidation. Who needs them? We all do. Who wants to escape them? We all do. That is, until we mature spiritually and begin to see the purpose of hardship, pain and trial from the Father's perspective. If we are to become the *"more than conquerors"* that is referred to by Paul in Romans 8:37, then we must trust God's use of the varieties of problems as His instruments, tools and sandpaper to spiritually develop and equip us to carry out our divine mission in the earth, with the ultimate goal of conforming us to the image of Christ.

No problem, pain or hardship can touch the life of a child of God without first touching the Father. What pierces our palms pierces His first. Your pain and suffering has already been experienced by Him at Calvary. The threshold question is, "Will you take up your cross and follow Him?" Or a more poignant question and answer set forth in an old gospel hymn is, *"Must Jesus bear the cross alone and all the world go free? No, there's a cross for everyone and there's a cross for me."*

The life of a child of God is the Way of the Cross. There is no question that the Way of the Cross is tough. But our God is tougher. No matter the origin of our suffering or trial, whether it be ordained by the Father, manufactured by Satan, or caused in some way by our own actions; God has the first and last say over the depth, breadth and length of our suffering or trial.

Once we begin to see Jesus Christ, rather than man, as the Architect of our affairs; and begin to see our excruciating circumstances as Christ-centered crucibles, we are less inclined to attempt to escape what the Father has designed for His glory and our ultimate good.

Imagine if you will that the Father has stored up boxes-upon-boxes-of-blessings with your name on them. However, the outer wrapping paper is made of storms, seasons of suffering, disappointment, sickness, betrayal, financial setbacks, loss of loved ones, or perhaps even a period of public disgrace.

When the delivery of abundant blessings from the Lord arrives at your door, because your vision is limited to a worldly perspective, you suffer from the condition of spiritual myopia. That just means you're unable to see beyond the outer wrapping of difficult experiences and discern the surprise blessing of the Father inside the package of some hardship or trial. Since you gave in to your inclination to escape the pain and suffering designed for you by the Father, the delivery of blessings can't be made because you've moved. You've escaped your old address of hardship, pain and trial. Or so you think.

But in time, and because the Father loves us so much, He again sends untold blessings wrapped in the storms and seasons of suffering and setbacks. Again, we have a choice. We can muster every ounce of faith and courage in us, and take up our cross and follow Jesus. Or we can deny Him, succumb to our escapist inclinations, brought on by the fear and trepidation of being crucified with Christ, and say, to paraphrase Peter, "...*Woman, I know him not*" (Luke 22:57).

"A High Cost Enterprise"

One of the best definitions of sin is that articulated by Dr. Tony Evans, Senior Pastor of Oak Cliff Bible Fellowship and President of The Urban Alternative. In describing sin as a high cost enterprise, Dr. Evans says: *"Sin takes you further than you want to go; keeps you longer than you want to stay; and makes you spend more than you intended to pay."*

We commit sin every time we are disobedient to God in some form or fashion. How can we know for sure? We must use our sacred privilege of reading and meditating on the Word of God. We must also develop a spiritual sensitivity to the work of the Holy Spirit that speaks to our hearts and pricks our consciences.

God has the big picture. He always has our back. He holds the blueprint for our life in his Hand. He and He alone, knows what is best for us, under any circumstances. When we pursue a life of sin, it's as if we have classified God as an incompetent and know-nothing. Our sinful actions say to God, "What do you know? I'm in charge here."

In no uncertain terms, the Bible teaches us: *"For the wages of sin is death; but the gift of God is eternal life through Jesus Christ our Lord."* (Romans 6:23). The Bible also instructs us in Romans 12: 19-21:

"Dearly beloved, avenge not
yourselves, but rather give place
unto wrath: for it is written,
vengeance is mine; I will
repay, saith the Lord.

"Therefore if thine enemy
hunger, feed him; if he thirst,
give him drink: for in so doing
thou shalt heap coals of fire on his head."
"Be not overcome of evil, but
overcome evil with good."

We don't always die a physical death. But we die on the inside. We die spiritually, because sin pollutes the soul. And if we sin often enough and long enough, our soul becomes twisted out of shape, numb, and unrecognizable to our spirit. And, without our soul, we become the walking dead.

Think of all of the walking dead that you have encountered on the path of life. They hold jobs. They bear children. They run companies. They diagnose medical conditions and prescribe medicines. They sing and dance on stage. They become elected to political office. They don black robes and judge others. But "their eyes are dead and they are dead behind them." *Sin has seared their consciences and caused them to lose their souls.*

A story recently appeared in the local newspaper about a 38-year-old woman who finally admitted to arranging for the murder of her business partner. She had given him a quarter of a million dollars to secure a multimillion dollar contract for her company. He had neither delivered the contract nor returned her money.

She then hired a hit man and together they conspired and killed her partner. Her partner's death would then allow her to collect a quarter of a million dollars as the beneficiary of one of his life insurance policies. Here is a classic case of sin having taken this woman further than she wanted to go; kept her longer than she wanted to stay; and made her spend more than she intended to pay.

It is always unwise to judge the motives and actions of another in a given set of circumstances when we are not privy to all the facts. However, I am certain that if this dear woman could live this part of her life over again, knowing what she knows now; she would not hesitate for a moment to turn the whole matter over to God to handle according to His divine plan and purpose for her life and the life of her partner.

Now having to endure all the consequences of her actions, if she could roll back the clock, she would most likely, in the face of the same set of circumstances, be willing to allow God, a man who does not lie, to teach her three colossal truths. The first truth is: *"Be not deceived; God is not mocked: for whatsoever a man soweth, that shall he also reap"* (Galatians 6:7). Or in the words of Dr. Charles Stanley, "He shall reap what he sows, more than he sows and later than he sows." The second truth is that "*Vengence is mine saith the Lord, I will repay*" (Romans 12:19). And the third truth, so eloquently expressed by Dr. Mike Murdock, is: "*Whatever we're willing to walk away from determines what God will bring to us.*"

God does not bring greed, death and destruction. Satan does. And he does so by convincing us that we can fulfill our needs by any means necessary. In other words, we let the Devil convince us that the end always justifies the means—a lie straight from the pit of hell.

If all of our thoughts, words and actions are not consistent with the Word of God, we are destined for big trouble sooner or later. Therefore, it behooves each one of us to stop and consider our thoughts, words and deeds. We must make it a priority to seek the wisdom and guidance of the Holy Spirit in our daily walks and talks with our fellow man.

If you will make it a habit to first pray before you proceed, God will, at all times and in all ways, protect you, preserve you, prosper you and "*exalt you at the proper time*" and in the proper way. You will not have to align yourself with the enemy to have your needs met. You will not have to pay the high cost of sin.

"This, This, This And That"

One of my favorite gospel songs, sung by one of our area churches in their television broadcast, includes the following lyrics in its refrain:

"Whatever the problem,
I'll put it all in His hand.

My God, He can solve them;
I'll put it all in His hand.

This, this, this and that;
I'll put it all in His hand."

Nothing could be truer. Whatever your problem, God can solve it. And most of our problems can be summed up in one of four categories: *this, this, this and that.* This disappointment over here. This setback over there. This hardship out there. That loss back there. My alcoholic mate over here. My prodigal son out there. My interfering in-laws over here. My over-bearing boss out there. My unfaithful spouse over here. That unjust judge down there. My disloyal friend out there. My betraying colleague back there. My rebellious daughter in here. My deceptive client out there.

No problem is too hard for God. In fact, God has permitted the problem we are facing to challenge us to look to Him, and Him only, for its solution. Spiritually, "how we see the problem is the problem." Our problems are divinely designed for our spiritual growth and maturation. They are not designed to defeat, embarrass, humiliate, ridicule or disgrace us. Rather, they are designed to usher us into our promised land.

If we see the problem as outside of God's will for our life, and one that we must solve all by ourselves, then that is the problem. But if we see the problem, to borrow a phrase from Pastor and bestselling author, Rick Warren, as being "Father-filtered," coming straight from the hand of the Father, our whole life will be radically transformed in line with God's will for our life.

When that happens, we would be well advised to fasten our seat belts, because the blessings from above will begin to pour in. They will begin to chase us down and overtake us. (Deuteronomy 28:2). In *"...good measure, pressed down, and shaken together, and running over, shall men give into your bosom"* (Luke 6:38).

We shall find that not only is God a Man who cannot lie, but He is constantly taking us through a personal practicum, uniquely tailored-made for us, to prove the reality of His promises to His children.

If viewed rightly, the experience of problems serves to teach us, as nothing else, what it means to trust and obey the Lord. Moreover, overcoming a problem deepens our faith in God's omnipotence, omniscience and omnipresence. The next time we are faced with a giant of a problem, we will surprisingly find ourselves responding in a calm, cool, confident and Christ-like manner.

We are then well on our way to experiencing, from the Father's perspective, the perfect solutions to our problems. We are also well on our way of becoming a better person for having overcome our problems through the testimony of the Holy Spirit that resides within us. We shall then be able to say with Paul, *"Nay, in all these things we are more than conquerors through him that loved us"* (Romans 8:37).

Wisdom Is A Woman

Every child of God has been spiritually gifted with special talents, skills and abilities. However, every daughter of the King has been uniquely endowed with the gift of wisdom. And so it can be said that, "*Wisdom is a woman.*" I learned this truth from a variety of women all around me, all of my life. These included my mother, my grandmother, my many aunts on both sides of the family, especially my mother's younger sister, Blanche Bailey. My life was also positively impacted by my mother's many friends from her childhood, especially Annie Robinson, her best friend and contemporary confidant; Ruth Royal, Juanita Cavanaugh, Bertha Hollis and Bessie March.

Other women who served as unforgettable role models in my life were the teachers, administrators and executive staff of the Fuld Neighborhood House in Newark where my brothers and I spent countless hours after school and in the summer when we were not away at summer camp in Kingston, New York. These educators and mentors included, but were by no means limited to, Dr. Antoinette Fried, Suzanne Zimmer, Helen Reid, Geraldine Smith, Mrs. Grayson, Ann Oliver and Mrs. Dorsey. Lastly, I shall always be grateful for my piano teachers, Mrs. Gold, and Mrs. DeDeaux, both of whom provided excellent instruction and coached me for my many piano recitals and my annual participation in the Griffith Piano Auditions held each year in the City of Newark. And finally, I shall always be grateful to the many women officers, members, class leaders and lay organization members of the St. Luke A.M.E. Church, under the auspices of the First Episcopal District of the African Methodist Episcopal Church.

However, it was my grandmother, more than any other, who represented the spiritual truth that "*Wisdom is a woman.*" When I had a problem that needed to be untangled; or an issue that needed to be first understood in order to be resolved; I would go to Mama for her godly advice and counsel.

When I arrived at Mama's house, I would usually find her in the kitchen. No matter how burdened I would be or how heavy my problem, Mama would continue doing whatever she was doing when I arrived. Whether she was cooking, or washing dishes, or sweeping, or mopping the kitchen floor, Mama would keep right on doing what she was doing, while I talked. Nevertheless, she would hear me out completely, having listened intently to all I had to say.

After I had divulged all sides of my problem to Mama, she would, in an even, confident and unequivocal voice say, "Well, the Bible tells us that..." and then Mama would quote verbatim an appropriate scripture that served as God's answer to either how to resolve a particular problem or how not to resolve it. Mama's knowledge of the Scriptures was extensive and accurate. She had, for over fifty years, memorized most of the books of the Bible. David's Psalms were her favorite. Mama's mastery and memory of Scripture was not only impressive, but impeccable. If Mama said it, I could believe it.

We would then discuss that particular Scripture as God's Word to me in addressing my problem. Sometimes Mama would share her own life experiences in helping to shed light on my situation.

But even more than Mama's confident tone, was her staunch attitude of faith that there was nothing that I faced or confronted me that the Almighty, working through me, could not overcome and conquer. Mama would always assure me, "If you will just hold yourself together, stand firm and trust God, He will bring you out *'more than conquered'*" *(Romans 8:37)*.

The precious and invaluable lesson that Mama was teaching me was that it would be my willingness to allow the Holy Spirit to work through me as He saw fit; to be obedient to His commands, and to leave all the consequences to Him. I look forward to reuniting with Mama in glory and telling her she was absolutely right.

Long before I became a teenager, Mama had pointed me to the Word of God for everything. Years later, as a young adult, I realized that Mama was again pointing me to that *"wisdom that is from above is first pure, then peaceable, gentle, and easy to be intreated, full of mercy and good fruits, without partiality, and without hypocrisy"* *(James 3:17)*.

If we will examine our life, most of us have godly women in our lives who, because of their knowledge of the Word and commitment to live a holy life, are full of wisdom from above which, when shared, can lead us into a spiritual understanding of the challenges we face and a peace that passes all understanding.

Putting Pain In Its Place

One of the reasons our seasons of pain and suffering take us to deeper depths as opposed to higher heights as they are divinely intended to do is that we fail to put pain in its place. Consequently, our times of pain are usually more severe than they need to be. We put pain in its place when we see it as coming from the hand of a loving Father Almighty, the creator of this universe and all that is therein.

It behooves us to begin to spiritually see the place of pain as a sacred and holy place — a place of sweet communion with our Lord. Nothing gets God's attention faster than the excruciating pain being experienced by one of His children. Our painful times, however they are caused, are times when we are most susceptible to hearing the still small voice of the Holy Spirit, if we would only take the time to be still and listen.

Very often our pain is prodigal. In some area of our life, we have either chosen to live recklessly, spend lavishly, or give foolishly. The bottom line is that we have squandered our spiritual, and therefore, material inheritance. The wasteful expenditure of our time, talent and treasure is the consequence of our prodigal living. It is allowed by the Father.

We demand our inheritance. The Father accommodates our request. We rebel against the Father. The Father remains in the Father's house. We choose the street and its gutters over the Father's house on the hill. The street demands our inheritance in exchange for a mess of potash and riotous living. Once we have been stripped of all that was ours by Divine Right from the Father, employment in the pig pen is all that is available to us. As far as the pigs are concerned, we are one of them. Our former consorts and cohorts on the street don't even remember our name.

Our success and fulfillment in the Father's House is but a dream faintly remembered. The author, L.B. Cowman, agrees with me on this issue of putting pain in its place when she says, "If you want to achieve victory and peace and the ability to put pain in its place, you must begin to see everything coming from the hand of God" (Op. Cit., p. 193).

"The World Is Waiting For You"

Most people find it difficult to believe, and might even consider it arrogant to suggest that *"The world is waiting to be ennobled by our fullest participation."* However, author Sandra Felton boldly puts forth this very truth as one of the foundational themes in her outstanding instructional manual entitled *The New Messies Manual* (Fleming H. Revell: Grand Rapids, MI, 2000, p. 74).

Each of us has been given the means by our heavenly Father, through a special gift and talent that, if exercised to its fullest, is designed to lift us and the rest of humanity, to the level of nobility. When we use fully our God-given talents and gifts, we are like "the tide that comes in and lifts all boats." God has created us to participate fully in life. He did not create us to follow the path of the message on a bumper sticker on the back of a car I saw in traffic: "I get up. I eat. I get dressed." Most of us would readily agree that this is a far cry from participating fully in life. But if we are working all day at the office and not working on our manuscript at night, but instead, are watching our television for hours at a time, we are not participating fully.

Even if we put in a full day every day at the office, and fail to discipline ourselves to take the time, here and there, to pursue what God is speaking to our hearts to do, we are not participating fully. In this regard, I am reminded of the statement made by the powerful Bible teacher, Oswald Chambers, when he said, "If we obey God, it is going to cost other people more than it costs us, and that is where the pain begins…We must let the cost be paid…If, however, we obey God, He will take care of those who have suffered the consequences of our obedience. We must simply obey and leave all the consequences with Him." (Chambers, Op. Cit., "January 11").

Are we getting "F's" instead of 'A's" in life because we are not participating fully; because we are functioning way below our potential? We are working in the company's kitchen when we should be sitting in its boardroom. We are enrolling in the classrooms of life when we should be seeking to be the administrators and members of the faculty. We are serving as teachers when God has called us to be principals, chancellors and textbook authors. We are employed as associate attorneys when we should be law partners. We are pastors' wives and co-pastors when we should be pastors, presiding elders and bishops.

The world was waiting for Jesus, and Esther, and Job, and Lazarus, and David, and George Washington Carver, and Margaret Mitchell, and Gwendolyn Brooks, and Leonard Bernstein and Richard Allen, and Aretha Franklin, and W.E.B. Dubois, and Rosa Parks, and Ella Fitzgerald, and Ralph Ellison, and Albert Einstein, and Ray Charles and Lucille Ball, and Frederick Douglass, and Eleanor Roosevelt, and Martin Luther King, Jr., and Harriet Tubman and John F. Kennedy, Jr., and Stevie Wonder.

And let no one fool you—the world is waiting for you.

God has given each of us gifts and talents that He expects us to use to the fullest. Phenomenal success is conditioned upon our full, and not partial, use of our God-given abilities and skills. Begin to move boldly in the direction of your unique gifts, and watch God work. He will uproot your most intransigent fears, calm your shuddering spirit and exalt you in ways that no man can.

Why not give him a try? He says, "*...and prove me now herewith, saith the Lord of hosts, if I will not open you the windows of heaven, and pour you out a blessing, that there shall not be room enough to receive it*" (Malachi 3:10).

The Power of Written Goals

"And the Lord answered me, and said, *'Write the vision, and make it plain upon tables, that he may run that readeth it. For the vision is yet for an appointed time, but at the end it shall speak, and not lie: though it tarry, wait for it; because it will surely come, it will not tarry.'" Habakkuk 2:2-3* In the words of the Prophet Habakkuk, we are instructed to write out our goals and make them specific. God has admonished us to write out our goals because He knows that He has designed the process of goal-setting in such a manner that incredible power is inherent in written goals.

Moreover, our written goals must be as specific as buying an airplane ticket. When we purchase a plane ticket, we must give specific information before the ticket is issued to us. We must know where we are going in order to identify the destination of our trip. We must know when we plan to travel so that we can give the departure date. We must identify the airport from which we shall depart, as well as the airport to which we would like to land. Lastly, we must identify the form of payment for the ticket. Imagine the frustration and confusion for all parties involved in making our travel arrangements, if we could not articulate the specifics of our trip.

This is what happens when we fail to write out our goals. It is as if we have come before the Father, who is able to give us more than we could ever ask, dream or imagine, but in our failure to write out our goals and make them specific, we tie the Father's hand to help us. We must see our written goals as prayers of petition to the Heavenly Father. It is the Father's desire to supply the resources that are needed in achieving our goals.

Whether the help that is needed consists of financial resources, the right contacts, resources of wisdom, creative ideas, godly personnel, the right business address, an abundance of clients or colleagues of commitment and integrity, there is no resource beyond the creative and omnipotent power of the Father. There is something that is almost magical about written goals as opposed to unwritten, although verbally declared, goals.

David Bach, in his national bestseller, "*Smart Women Finish Rich*," advises that until our goals are written down, they are not goals at all but mere slogans. (Broadway Books: New York, N.Y., 2002, p.72). It is not enough to be goal oriented. We must take the next step. We must write down our goals. God rewards those of us who write down our goals in ways that will astound us.

Written goals are actually our prayers to the Father to support our endeavors to achieve our goals, however feeble our initial attempts. God wants to help us in magnificent and wonderful ways. He has spoken through Habakkuk, giving us the specific command to write out our goals. It is our duty to obey the Word of God. It is our duty to dare to dream our impossible dreams. It is our duty to defy the odds and do the job that only we can do. It is our duty to bring glory and honor to God the Father, the Son and the Holy Spirit.

"My Work Is My Prayer"

It has been reported that Duke Ellington, the late, great American Jazz Composer, Pianist and Band Leader, in answering the question as to whether he prayed, paused for a moment, and then simply said, "My work is my prayer." It was for Duke and it is for each of us. After all has been said and done, at the end of the day, our work has been our prayer.

Duke Ellington had been created by God to create beautiful Jazz music that year-after-year continues to inspire and influence millions of people around the globe. His life is a portrait of one who had committed, against all odds, to walk in God's will for his life. And his work brought eternal glory to God and significant good and historical recognition to Duke and his African-American heritage.

Many years ago, I questioned the practical application of Paul's admonition to us to "*Pray without ceasing*" (I Thessalonians 5:17). "How would this be possible," I asked myself. After all, I have to work, meet with clients, shop for food, accomplish numerous household chores, and attend church services and social engagements with my husband. And the list goes on. As believers, are we to literally follow Paul's challenge to "*Pray without ceasing?*" With all due respect to Paul, "How could I make this happen in my life?"

And then one day, I don't remember exactly when, I realized that everything we do, including our work, is a form of prayer. Every time we go forward in some endeavor, recognizing that Jesus is walking beside us, we are praying. Every time we take a step in obedience to what God has told us to do, without knowing what the end will be, we are praying. Every time we trust God and wait, we are praying. Every time we resist the temptation to get ahead of the Holy Spirit, we are praying. Every time we stand immovable before the mountains in our lives, we are praying. Every time we endure, in total surrender to God, the fighting within and the fears without, we are praying. Every time we remain steadfast in the circumstances that come with the life God has called us to, we are praying.

Every time, in faith, we refuse to panic, we are praying. Every time we refuse to see obstacles as punishment and penalty, but as

God's opportunities for the demonstration of His power, we are praying. Every time, with Emerson, we "contemplate the facts of life from the highest point of view," we are praying. Every time, with Kipling, we "trust ourselves, when all men doubt us, and being lied about, don't deal in lies; or being hated, don't give way to hating," we are praying.

Each of us has been endowed and imbued with special gifts and talents that, when used according to God's will for our lives, enable us to humbly, albeit magnificently, carry out our divine assignment in the world. The Father regards our work as so sacred that, from His perspective, Duke had it right: our work is our prayer.

"Only Heaven Could Mess Up This Much"

In her New York Times Bestseller *"Anatomy of the Spirit,"* (Three Rivers Press: New York, 1996, pp. 125-127) the author and medical intuitive, Caroline Myss, Ph.D., tells the story of a man who had attended one of her workshops. Ten years earlier, his entire life had crashed. It had begun when his two business partners announced they no longer wanted to work with him. They made him an optional settlement offer. He could take a small cash payment or all of the stock in the company which was actually worthless.

He left the office stunned. When he arrived home, before he could tell his wife what had happened, she told him that she had met someone else and wanted a divorce. His summation of the day's events was classic and astute: All three of his partners had divorced him in one day. Although overwhelmed and an avowed atheist, he concluded that "only heaven could mess up someone's life this much." And so that night he prayed and asked God to tell him whether He was behind this. And if so, he would follow whatever direction God gave him.

That night he had a very vivid dream. Based on his interpretation of the dream, he decided to take his partners' offer of all the stock in their worthless company. He also knew that he had to release his business partners and his wife without anger. He had to say farewell to them, even though ironically, they thought they were getting rid of him.

Thereafter, a number of opportunities to help his company were presented. Although getting the business off the ground was rough during the early months, as the dream had foretold, he hung on because he knew, from the dream, that he would make it.

Today he describes himself as having one of the most successful companies in Belgium. He is also remarried to the most wonderful woman and life partner. He begins each day in prayerful praise and gratitude to God for separating him from his former wife and two business partners. When he meets someone who is experiencing a *down-to-nothing time*, he tells them: "God is behind you. There is nothing to worry about. I know that for a fact."

This case study reveals the man's immediate recognition of the operation of a higher hand in his affairs. His experience, albeit shocking and overwhelming, was the beginning of a spiritual transformation of his entire life. The details of the events were all woven into the tapestry of the Divine design for his life. The sin that he had been exposed to had been permitted by God, not to sink him but to sanctify him. He was able to realize, as did Joseph, that what his business partners and wife meant for evil, God intended for good (Genesis 50:20).

Therefore, the next time you find yourself deeply enmeshed in a real mess, don't panic. Know that it is your Maker that has intricately designed the details of your circumstances, however ostensibly hellish they may appear to be. God's hand on your life is one of unconditional love and wisdom. If you are patient and trusting, you will see wonderful, glorious results that could only come from the hands of the Master Potter. You will find that it will be your trust in Him that will treat your depression and any feelings of defeat and betrayal that assail you.

Your mess in the hands of the Heavenly Father will become the message of your ministry to a decaying and dying world.

When The Spoken Word Is Silence

Do you remember times when you have uttered words that you wish you would have never said? Perhaps it was a time when you were in the midst of some hardship or trial; a time when you were feeling particularly pressured, and a time when you were swamped by the cares of this world. Or it could have been a time when you simply failed to think before speaking. Yes, we have all been there and done that.

How often have we paid dearly or cost others dearly for words uttered needlessly, carelessly, or recklessly? My grandmother used to say, "It's not what's in you that hurts you. It's what comes out."

I recently heard someone share that he uses the analogy of a tube of toothpaste in teaching his children the concept of being unable to take back their spoken words. He had each child put toothpaste on his toothbrush. He then instructed them to put the toothpaste on their brush back into the tube. Notwithstanding their sincere and determined effort, the children were unable to put the toothpaste back into the tube.

While we can't take the words back we've spoken, and we must reap the fruit they spawn, no one, except the Holy Spirit, can charge us for words unsaid, even though in our heads. If the words in our minds are unlovely, unkind, profane or even hateful, we must ask God to forgive us and cleanse our hearts and minds of all that is in us that is not of His Spirit working in us. We must then discipline ourselves to think before we speak, speak if we must, or respond in silence.

The Bible teaches us that :

"A good man out of the good treasure of his heart bringeth forth that which is good; and an evil man out of the evil treasure of his heart, bringeth forth that which is evil: for of the abundance of the heart his mouth speaketh" (Luke 6:45).

And Paul characteristically challenges us in Phillipians 4:8:

"Finally brethren, whatsoever things are true, whatsoever things are honest, whatsoever things are just, whatsoever things are pure, whatsoever things are lovely, whatsoever things are of good report; if there be any virtue, and if there be any praise, think on these things."

Obedience to this command allows us to condition our minds in such a way that when we speak, we speak words that are approved of God, no matter what the setting.

God Okays Our Problems

Our problems are merely training exercises designed by God to develop and arm us with the spiritual and physical attributes we need to carry out our divine mission in the earth. Our problems are also our opportunities to appreciate the power and presence of God. As someone has aptly put it, *"If we didn't have problems, we wouldn't know that God could solve them."*

It would help tremendously if, when confronted with a problem, we would ask our self, "What is the lesson that God intends to teach me through the management and ultimate solution of this problem?" God molds each of us differently, depending on our unique assignment. Therefore, we should never envy nor begrudge others when it appears that our burdens are greater and heavier, or our lessons are more difficult and demanding.

Rather, we should keep our gaze fixed on the Master's unique, divine plan and purpose in using us in His Kingdom. This is a time to remember that the greater the burden, the greater the opportunity realized in *"casting all your care upon him, for he careth for you"* (I Peter 5:7).

God has made us for a unique and special purpose. We are designed to cultivate, and then share, our special gifts with others as servants of God and as ambassadors for Christ. God holds the playbook and blueprint of our lives in His hands. He knows all of the problems we shall encounter and endure.

Think of the biblical characters that faced untold problems, pressure and pain, but did not waver in their faith and trust in God to bring them through. When you are faced with a problem, know that it is the Almighty that has given the green light to your problem. The ball is now in your court, and God wants to see how you are going to respond; what you're going to do with the ball. Will you throw up your hands and say "Oh, God, what am I going to do?" Or will you respond rightly and let God hear you say "God, what are *You* going to do?" This question is like music to the ears of God. It is evidence that you are dependent on Him.

The proper perspective in managing our problems has been stated with deep wisdom and insight by the late, powerful Bible teacher, Oswald Chambers: "*If God has made your cup sweet, drink it with grace; or even if He has made it bitter, drink it in communion with Him.*" (*Updated Edition, My Utmost For His Highest*, Discovery House Publishers: Grand Rapids, Michigan, 1995). You are not leaning on your own understanding. You are trusting in God to help you learn all that you can from the problem. Further, you are trusting God to bring you out more than conquered, more determined, more sensitive to others, stronger, wiser, more forgiving, and more resolved to accomplish the work that God has assigned to you. Lastly, you are trusting that, in due season, God will promote you to the next level of your earthly mission.

Clutter Conundrum

Over the years, I have learned that when I am feeling fatigued for no apparent reason; when my energy is at an all time low; when it takes all the strength I can muster to go from left foot to right foot and then breathe, it is usually because I'm being weighed down—mentally, physically and emotionally—by all the clutter around me.

At these times, reflection and observation reveal that I am responding to the inherent negative impact of clutter in my life. I am surrounded by an over accumulation of things in my life that serve no other purpose than to hinder the full expression of my God-given abilities, talents and skills. Clutter, admittedly a difficult problem for many of us, results in what I call *clutter conundrum.*

Author Sandra Felton in *The New Messies Manual* (Grand Rapids, MI: Fleming H. Revell: 2000, p. 74) has astutely observed that "We are unique, valuable people. There is an orderly and effective individual within us. Our contribution to the world is being warped and dissipated by the clutter that hinders our full expression of our abilities. The world is waiting to be ennobled by our fullest participation."

Clutter acts as invisible handcuffs to our power to continually create vacuums for the new that wants to come into our lives: new relationships, new clothes, new books, new friends, new interests, new ideas, new prayers, new food, new furniture, new houses, new music, new vernacular and the sacrament of new work for our hands to do.

God has told us in His Word that He wants to do a new thing. In Isaiah 43:19 (Amplified), God tells us: *"Behold, I am doing a new thing; now it springs forth; do you not perceive and know it, and will you not give heed to it? I will even make a way in the wilderness and rivers in the desert."* But we tie God's hands, albeit unintentionally, when we have no room for God to work. God would like to work here, there and everywhere. But when He looks around, there is clutter here, there and everywhere. God cannot and will not create the new amidst the clutter. God is a God of order. We are made in his image and likeness. And that is why clutter tends to make us so uncomfortable and stressed out, if not absolutely crazy.

What is needed is the periodic invocation of *the vacuum law of life*. We invoke the vacuum law of creation of the new when we clean out our houses, our dresser drawers, our closets, our kitchen cabinets, our car trunks, our attics, our basements, our garages and last, but certainly not least, the headquarters of all clutter—our storage units. Finally, we make room for the new when we let go of stressful, draining and parasitic relationships.

Clear out of your life what is no longer of use to you; has never been of use to you or has rarely been of use to you. When you engage in this kind of clearing, you are invoking the vacuum law of creation. And since nature abhors a vacuum, watch how quickly those newly created spaces fill up. It is important that you ask God to fill the new space with what God has in store and wants to send into your life. You'll find that this adventure is nothing less than extraordinary in the arena of relationships.

Some years ago, I watched a television broadcast of a church service of the then popular and widely known Reverend Ike of New York City. During the service he interviewed a lovely husband and wife who were members of his congregation. During their testimony, the congregation and television audience learned that they had met and married, in large part, as a result of Reverend Ike's counseling of the wife. The spiritual principles taught by Reverend Ike included, among others, the principle of the vacuum law and its practical application to one's daily life in the achievement of personal goals consistent with God's plan and purpose for one's life.

The wife, prior to her marriage, had expressed to Rev. Ike her desire for marriage and a husband. Rev. Ike then asked her what was the state of her closets at home. Did she have any room in her closets for a mate's clothing? Her immediate reaction was to laugh and admit that her closets were jammed packed with her own clothing.

Rev. Ike said that her closets declared that she presently had no room in her life for a husband. He advised her to go home and clear some closet space for the wardrobe of her future husband. She followed his advice to the letter. Not long after, she met and married the wonderful man that God sent into her life. None of this could have occurred without her clearing the clutter and creating a vacuum for the new that she so wanted to come into her life.

This true story serves as a lesson for all of us in addressing the issue of clutter in our lives. Clutter is anathema to the clay that the Master Potter holds in Hands, ready and eager to create anew in our lives all that we could ever dream or imagine.

"Stick To It In Spite Of Hell And Other People"

If you are a follower of Christ, then it is fair to assume that you are a praying person. You are regularly in conversation with God. If you are in regular dialogue with God, He is instructing you as to the way you should go concerning your Christian journey.

Whether your journey consists of twists and turns, uphill climbs and downhill plunges, sudden stops, long stretches of desert roads, and roller coaster rides that leave you out of breath and begging to get off, God is still with you and speaking to you at every moment.

God is always speaking to us, but so is hell and other people. God says "Launch out into the deeps." Other people say, "Are you crazy?" Hell says, "You know you can't swim." Our five senses tell us, "No way." Katherine Anne Porter, in encouraging would-be authors, is reported to have said, *"Stick to it in spite of hell and other people."*

Jesus tells us to *"Come."* But we hang back. He continues calling. We continue hanging back. We won't admit it, but we're simply afraid to follow Christ. We've substituted the counsel of mere humans for the counsel of the all knowing and all mighty God.

We entrust futures and blessings to those whom God has not spoken on our behalf; to those whose ears and eyes are not spiritually trained to hear *"Thus, saith the Lord."* We all have people in our lives who are well meaning in their efforts to steer us in the right direction. But when one is on the threshold of making important decisions that will determine where we shall spend eternity, it is the voice of God spoken to the intended recipient that must take center stage; while the counsel of others, however well-intentioned, must be marked and stamped, "Return to Sender."

When we are operating under orders, God expects us to hold fast and remain faithful to His Word. He expects us to never give in, give out, or give up, until His purpose has been accomplished in our lives and the lives of others that we touch in carrying out our divine assignment.

God will test our obedience to His Word and special instruction by allowing the Adversary to have temporary triumph in the midst of our circumstances. When these times come, we must not become discouraged or depressed by *the vicissitudes of the game of life*. Our God is still in control and not one scintilla of evil can touch the child of God without the sovereign will and unconditional love of the Father.

Mother and I were blessed with the privilege of hearing, once again, the Word of God preached by the Rev. Dr. Lee P. Washington, Senior Pastor of Reid Temple A.M.E. Church in Glenn Dale, Maryland at the March, 2007 communion service. The sermonic topic indicated on the printed program was *"Faithing Your Future."* However, when Pastor Washington rose to speak, He announced to the congregation that the Holy Spirit had told him to change the topic to *"I'm Sticking With God."* In characteristic dynamic and inspiring fashion, Dr. Washington then preached a powerful message on the faith demonstrated by Jesus—a faith that did not waver, but remained steadfast in the midst of evil tidings by the Pharisees—a faith that courageously declared: *"I'm sticking with God"* (Luke 13:31-35).

When our time comes to experience a gut wrenching trial; when season after season brings nothing but setbacks, drenching rains and howling wind storms; when, so exhausted from the battle, we are ready to give up; if we will respond from a godly point of view of our circumstances, we shall learn that these can be the most precious, productive and powerful times in our lives.

For it is at these times that, if we keep our eyes on the Master, He is able to take us to that secret place in God where our tongues become speechless, but our hearts burn within us while He walks with us by the way side. When we come out of the secret place, we do so with an anointing that is so on fire for God, that God is able to use us in mighty and magnificent ways for the Kingdom.

"One More Move"

In *The Rainbow Connection,* (Unity School of Christianity: Unity Village, Missouri, 1983) the author, Rebecca Clark, tells the story of two young men on a transcontinental flight, engrossed in a game of chess. During what appeared to be a stalemate, an older passenger, sitting in an adjoining seat, became intrigued by the game. As one of the players was about to concede the game, the man gently touched his arm and said, "Wait! Look carefully at the board. *There is one more move you can make!*"

In response, the young player offered the man his place at the board. The man made one deft move that changed the perspective of the game. A few more quick maneuvers and the game was won! The man smiled, while the young players stared at each other in amazement. "When playing chess," he told them, "one more move may not always be possible."

However, *in the game of life,* when everyone's best efforts are seemingly insufficient to avert defeat, *there is always one more move*: letting go, giving total control of the situation to God and asking divine wisdom to solve the problem. (Op. Cit., pp. 212-213).

Some years later, the young player who was about to concede the game was called into the armed services during a time of war. Upon his return home, he shared an unforgettable experience while on active duty. He was cut off from his company in a foreign land, alone at night in a cold and damp foxhole, with enemy patrols approaching.

Enshrouded in fear for his life, he suddenly remembered the chess game and the man's admonition that there is always one more move. "He breathed a deep sigh and then prayed a prayer he will never forget. He implored God to take over his desperate situation. God answered. The tables turned! Under the cover of darkness, he surprised the enemy patrol, causing them to surrender. His one move of allowing God to take charge turned a seemingly impossible situation into a life-saving occurrence, including his own!" (Op. Cit., pp.213-214).

None of us is exempt from those circumstances and situations in life where we are surrounded by threatening appearances. We are ready to throw in the towel, to call it quits. We are ready to declare: "I don't need this. I've had enough of this already. This isn't living. This is just existing. I deserve more. I'm out of here!"

But these times must be viewed as opportune times to make one more move. And that move is the surrender of our entire life and all that touches and concerns us into the loving hands of the Holy Father. "We must trust God's heart, even though we don't see His hand."

Promise yourself that you will not go one more day without making one more move in that area of your life where victory is about to take a back seat to defeat. You will never regret that you made "*one more move.*"

Conclusion

I pray that I have accomplished in this work,
above all else, what I consider to be my
God-given assignment of pointing you
to the Incomparable Jesus Christ;
the God who is more than enough;
the One who has promised that if you
will ask anything in His Name, if He
does not have it, He will make it for you.

May God Richly Bless You,

Barbara Washington Franklin, Esq.

Acknowledgements

My Mother
Eunice Vetta Ross Washington
For A Lifetime of Tangible and Intangible
Support and Encouragement

My Daughter
Regan Alexandria Perry
For Quietly and Persistently Cheering
Me On This Writing Journey

My Son-in-Law
Kevin Anthony Perry
For Generously Sharing His Knowledge
Of Computer Science and Technology

My Friend
Rhonda Scarborough, Esq.
For Critically Reading the Manuscript
And Standing With Me In Prayer

My Friend
Joan Shingles Emory
For Agreeing With Me Years Ago
That I Would Finish and Publish This Manuscript

Ebony Magazine
For Its Gracious Permission To Use Its Photograph
For The Book's Cover

About The Author

B etween the ages of six and eight years old, the author and trial attorney, Barbara Washington Franklin, walked down the aisle of the St. Luke A.M.E. Church in Newark, joined the church and surrendered her life to Christ.

She was born in Blakely, Georgia and reared by her parents and grandparents in the Central Ward of Newark, New Jersey. She is a product of the Newark Public School System. She was the Valedictorian of her Cleveland Junior High School Class. At the age of sixteen, and during her Junior Year at Barringer High School, she was selected as one of five finalists in a student essay contest sponsored by the Newark Chapter of the United Nations Association. She was awarded, along with five other finalists, a 56-Day-Trip-Around-The-World, and traveled as an American Youth Goodwill Ambassador to seventeen (17) foreign countries throughout Europe, the Middle East, Far East and Asia. In preparation for the trip, she was mentored by the late Mrs. Eleanor Roosevelt.

She is an Honors graduate of Barringer High School; a graduate of Douglass College, the Women's College of Rutgers University; and a graduate of the Rutgers University Law School.

She is a former Newark and Philadelphia Public School Teacher; a New Jersey State Foster Care and Adoptions Social Worker; a Member of the American Peace Corps; a New York City Corporation Counsel Attorney; a NBC Senior Commercial Policy Editor; a U.S. Congressional Chief Counsel (Minority) and Staff Director; a District of Columbia Government Official and the Founder of the

Law Offices of Barbara Washington Franklin, a general civil litigation law practice.

She has been featured as an outstanding business woman and top attorney in various magazines and newspapers, including *Ebony Magazine*, *Vogue Magazine*, the *Washington Afro-American Newspaper*, and the *Washington Woman Magazine*.

The author resides with her family in Washington, D.C.

Contact With The Author

The author welcomes comments from her readers regarding
When You're Down to Nothing, God Is Up To Something.
You may contact her at the office address indicated below.

SPEAKING ENGAGEMENTS

The author is also available for speaking engagements.
You may contact her directly at her office address
indicated below.

Barbara Washington Franklin, Esq.
Chevy Chase Pavilion
5335 Wisconsin Avenue, N.W.
Suite 440
Washington, D.C. 20015
202-895-2780 (Office)
202-362-6969 (Facsimile)
Barbara.Washington Franklin@verizon.net

Printed in the United States
135817LV00003B/17/P

9 781606 471203